M000100502

"When Southern Baptists voluntarily work in partnership through the Cooperative ministries of the SBC, we are following a pattern found in Scripture. It is a pattern that allows us truly to do more together than we could ever do apart. It is a pattern that is biblically justified, theologically sound and practically wise. It involves the sacrificial giving of our financial resources, to be sure, but it is so much more than this. This is the argument my colleague and friend Scott Hildreth makes in *Together on God's Mission: How Southern Baptists Cooperate to Fulfill the Great Commission*. He is quite successful in his assignment."

—*Daniel L. Akin, president, Southeastern Baptist Theological Seminary*

"The cooperative partnership of Southern Baptists may not be perfect, but it is proven and profound. In *Together on God's Mission*, Scott Hildreth provides a timely resource that not only advocates for the financial wisdom of the Southern Baptists' Cooperative Program but also advances the theological foundation of this cooperative partnership for a new generation. As an experienced missionary and seminary professor, Hildreth provides a concise and helpful orientation of how churches unite to form a mighty Great Commission coalition as they join together on God's mission."

—*Brian Autry, executive director, SBC of Virginia*

"From their earliest days, Baptist churches have cooperated together for the sake of kingdom priorities such as missions, education, and public engagement. As Southern Baptists, we cooperate through our structures and strategy, which are linked together in the Cooperative Program. Every generation brings new challenges and fresh opportunities, and as this happens, pastors and other leaders need to be reminded anew of the importance of gospel-centered cooperation among churches of 'like faith and order' (as old-fashioned Baptists used to say). To that end, Scott Hildreth has written a book for such a time as this. *Together on God's Mission* gives us the perfect combination of Baptist history, sound biblical exegesis, missional theology, and constructive application."

—*Nathan A. Finn, dean, School of Theology and Missions, and professor of Christian thought and tradition, Union University*

"Scott Hildreth has done Southern Baptists a great service by providing this book. Of particular help, in my mind, is his commitment to help the SBC ground their partnership in theology rather than pragmatics. If you are Southern Baptist and care about cooperative mission, you should read this book."

—*Micah Fries, senior pastor, Brainerd Baptist Church, Chattanooga, TN*

"The perfect primer for getting your mind around the Cooperative Program—its unique opportunities, current challenges, and the way forward. Dr. Hildreth brings to this book an understanding that comes from years of working inside the system and the passion from having depended on the Cooperative Program while he served on the front lines of global missions."

—*J. D. Greear, pastor, The Summit Church, Raleigh-Durham, NC*

"In this informative book, Scott Hildreth shares from the rich knowledge he has gained as an IMB missionary and a professor of missions at a Southern Baptist seminary. With a succinct overview of how the Southern Baptist Convention came into being and grew to become the strongest Protestant missionary force in existence, Hildreth champions the benefit of a missions funding system that Southern Baptists know as the Cooperative Program. *Together on God's Mission* explains why cooperation and personal involvement in missions is the heartbeat of who Southern Baptists have been and still remain. Hildreth's work also reveals how those who hold to Baptist distinctives along with their personal convictions can work together in fulfilling the Great Commission. He reminds us that we can function most effectively in reaching the nations when we seek unity under our common statement of faith and around our common cooperative vision. Readers will benefit greatly from Hildreth's book, whether or not they grew up in a Southern Baptist church."

—*Milton A. Hollifield Jr., executive director-treasurer, Baptist State Convention of North Carolina*

"In the backward horizon of the Southern Baptist Convention, we can see dark clouds of human sin, but we can also see the lightning of God's grace. In *Together on God's Mission*, Scott Hildreth shows us how to spot such grace, and how to respond with gratitude. The book will help a new generation of Baptist Christians learn from our past in order to forge a future of cooperation for mission."

—*Russell Moore, president, the Ethics and Religious Liberty Commission of the Southern Baptist Convention*

"In *Together on God's Mission*, Scott Hildreth demonstrates that our convention priorities and our Cooperative Program are not only practical; they are biblical. This book tells the story of the development of Southern Baptist cooperation and shows how our structure and vision fits within God's global mission. It is well researched and accessible. I commend this book as a valuable tool for students, missionaries, pastors, as well as the masses of Southern Baptists across our convention who are called to share in God's mission of making disciples of all nations."

—*Ed Stetzer, Billy Graham Professor of Church, Mission, and Evangelism, and executive director of the Billy Graham Center for Evangelism, Wheaton College*

TOGETHER ON
GOD'S
MISSION

TOGETHER ON
GOD'S
MISSION

HOW SOUTHERN BAPTISTS
COOPERATE *to* FULFILL
the GREAT COMMISSION

D. SCOTT HILDRETH

ACADEMIC

NASHVILLE, TENNESSEE

Together on God's Mission:
How Southern Baptists Cooperate to Fulfill the Great Commission

Copyright © 2018 by Darren Scott Hildreth
Published by B&H Academic
Nashville, Tennessee
All rights reserved.

ISBN: 978-1-4336-4394-1

Dewey Decimal Classification: 286
Subject Heading: SOUTHERN BAPTIST CONVENTION--HISTORY \ SOUTHERN BAP-
TIST CHURCHES \ CHURCH

Scripture quotations marked CSB have been taken from the Christian Standard Bible®, Copyright
© 2017 by Holman Bible Publishers. Used by permission. Christian Standard Bible® and CSB® are
federally registered trademarks of Holman Bible Publishers.

The web addresses referenced in this book were live and correct at the time of the book's publication
but may be subject to change.

Printed in the United States of America
2 3 4 5 6 7 8 9 10 • 23 22 21 20 19 18
VP

Contents

Acknowledgments xiii

Abbreviations xv

Introduction 1

Part I

The Historical Development of the Southern Baptist Convention | 5

1. From Missionary Society to a Convention of Churches 7

2. The SBC Adopts a Cooperative Identity 15

3. How Southern Baptists Cooperate on Mission 25

Part II

God's Mission and the Mission of His People | 41

4. Our God Is a Missionary God 49

5. God's Mission and God's People 55

6. The Early Church and Its Cooperative Mission 65

PART III

SOUTHERN BAPTISTS: A PEOPLE PURSUING GOD'S MISSION | 73

7. A Proposal for Southern Baptist Cooperation. 75

8. Study Questions 85

9. Name Index 89

   Subject Index. 91

   Scripture Index. 93

To Lesley

To Rachel and Jacob

Acknowledgments

S ome say writing is a lonely task. This may indeed be true, but this book is the product of group effort. I do not write this to lay any responsibility for mistakes or bad writing on anyone else. Any errors are mine alone. However, this book is the result of the encouragement, prayer, and dedication of a large group of people.

First, I am grateful to the Southern Baptists. I dedicated this project, not only to Lesley, Rachel, and Jacob (see dedication), but to you. The Lord has used this convention to make me who I am. This book is an attempt to repay a debt.

Second, I am grateful to the faculty and staff at Southeastern Seminary. I am especially grateful to Steve McKinion and Greg Mathias for their patience, encouragement, prayers, and long conversations during this writing process. As well, I am grateful to Keith Harper and Amy Whitfield, who encouraged me along the way and were available to answer my questions.

Third, I cannot begin to express my appreciation to Danny Akin for his help. We have worked on this project on four continents, and in the air between them! The president of a seminary has dozens of distractions and outside commitments; however, he has always made time to provide help along the way. Without him, this would be an incomplete idea.

A special thanks to Ashley Clayton of the SBC Executive Committee, who helped me understand SBC reporting and statistics.

Finally, to my family: Mom and Dad, thanks for making sure I kept my head and kept the faith. To my children, Rachel and Jacob, thanks for all the mocking, prodding, and even your simple encouragement along the way. And finally, to my sweet wife, Lesley, only you know the sacrifice you have made. Without your encouragement, I would have never started; and without your continued encouragement, I could not have finished. "Thanks" is not enough, but that is all I can give here!

Abbreviations

BECNT	Baker Exegetical Commentary on the New Testament
NAC	The New American Commentary
NICNT	The New International Commentary on the New Testament
TDNT	*Theological Dictionary of the New Testament*

INTRODUCTION

The Southern Baptist Convention has a rich heritage of cooperation. In fact, cooperation has been a hallmark of Southern Baptist identity since its earliest days. In 1845, Baptists from the southern United States gathered in Augusta, Georgia, and established a convention of churches for the express purpose of "eliciting, combining, and directing the energies of the Baptist denomination of Christians for the propagation of the gospel."[1] In the years that followed, Southern Baptists developed a convention structure and identity that strengthened cooperation among churches and furthered this mission. Despite more than a century and a half of world crises, denominational conflict, and changes in convention leadership and structure, cooperation remains a defining feature of Southern Baptist life. This book tells the story, and describes the work, of Southern Baptist cooperation. It also shows how the Southern Baptist Convention is uniquely positioned to fully engage in God's global mission.

In 2005, Chad Brand and David Hankins wrote *One Sacred Effort: The Cooperative Program of the Southern Baptist Convention*. This book has been used for more than a decade to teach Southern Baptist seminarians, pastors, and laypersons about the inner working and vision of the Cooperative Program (CP) as the unified funding mechanism for the ministries and missionary advance of Southern Baptists in this country and around the world. *One Sacred Effort* was important for Southern Baptists because it showed how the Cooperative Program remained an important tool as Southern Baptists recovered from denominational conflict and headed into a new millennium. Much has changed within the Southern Baptist Convention since 2005. These changes have created an opportunity for a new book on Southern Baptist cooperation.

---

[1] This statement is taken from the preamble of the original constitution of the Southern Baptist Convention. It has become a popular phrase and even a rallying cry for Southern Baptists over the years.

I wrote this book to address the needs of a new generation. *Together on God's Mission* traces Southern Baptist history, showing how and why we came to embrace this vision of a cooperative convention of churches. It also explores how this vision shapes denominational identity and structure. This historical study is followed by a biblical and theological section exploring how God's mission shapes the mission of the church. This section demonstrates that cooperation among churches is a key component of God's mission to redeem the nations and restore creation from the effects of the fall.

Though the idea of cooperation is a hallmark of Southern Baptist identity, it has been difficult to agree on exactly what "being cooperative" requires. For example, Baptist historian Bill Leonard argued that in the early twentieth century, Southern Baptist cooperation was essentially financial. He wrote, "To be Southern Baptist was to practice stewardship the Southern Baptist way."[2] Many Southern Baptists still appear to understand cooperation this way, maintaining that it should be measured entirely by financial support of the Cooperative Program. Others allege this definition is reductionist. In 2014, David Platt was elected president of the International Mission Board (IMB). One of the main criticisms leveled against the trustees for their election of Platt was that the congregation he pastored, the Church at Brook Hills, did not give enough through the Cooperative Program. Though the church made significant contributions to Southern Baptist Convention (SBC) causes, their use of alternate funding pathways was described as uncooperative.[3] North Carolina pastor J. D. Greear addressed this concern: "David has wrestled with the CP, but not because he doesn't believe in cooperating in missions. *Because he does. . . .* It's not news that the younger generation of Southern Baptists struggle with denominational loyalty, expressed in CP giving."[4] As we can see, Southern Baptists agree it is important to cooperate but differ on what this means.

These struggles seem to have, at least in part, contributed to a decline in Cooperative Program support as a percentage of churches' undesignated receipts. In

[2] Bill Leonard, "Stewardship Promotion in the Southern Baptist Convention Since 1900," *Baptist History and Heritage* (1986): 8.

[3] According to a 2014 Baptist Press article by David Roach and Art Toalston, under David Platt's leadership, the Church at Brook Hills gave $25,000 through CP each of the five calendar years leading up to Platt's election as IMB president. In 2013, the congregation gave $300,000 to the IMB's Lottie Moon Christmas Offering for International Missions and $100,000 through the SBC Executive Committee for the SBC Cooperative Program Allocation Budget. Gifts sent directly to the Executive Committee rather than through a Baptist state convention are defined as designated gifts, not CP giving. David Roach and Art Toalston, "Cooperation Central to Platt's Vision at IMB," Baptist Press, August 27, 2014, http://www.bpnews.net/43240/cooperation-central-to-platts-vision-at-imb.

[4] J. D. Greear, "What David Platt's IMB Presidency Signals about our Future," the J. D. Greear Ministries website, August 27, 2014, http://www.jdgreear.com/my_weblog/2014/08/what-david-platts-imb-presidency-signals-about-our-future.html. Emphasis in original.

While Greear is certainly correct about the struggle some younger Southern Baptists have with the Cooperative Program, it is important to remember that CP percentages have been declining for more than 40 years. The current situation results from multiple generations deemphasizing Cooperative Program giving through Southern Baptist churches.

the 1981–82 fiscal year (the first year churches reported their undesignated receipts to the convention), Southern Baptist churches contributed an average of 10.7 percent of those receipts through the CP. By 2014–15, the percentage had decreased to 5.18 percent.[5] This decrease has been a cause for alarm. In fact, this downward trend reached such proportions that Tom Elliff, past president of the International Mission Board, asked, "Have we really concluded that we can accomplish more by ourselves than we can together?"[6] Many Southern Baptists seem to be reassessing the means, method, and motivation for cooperation within our convention. The history of our convention has demonstrated that there are significant practical benefits of working together; however, these no longer seem compelling for a growing population of Southern Baptists.

As we consider the mission of the Southern Baptist Convention into the twenty-first century, it is helpful to understand where we have come from. Historian Leon McBeth has observed that "the 'delegates' who met in Augusta, Georgia in May 1845 to form the Southern Baptist Convention would hardly recognize their creation today.... The name remains, but almost everything else has changed."[7] Part 1 of this book traces the development of the Southern Baptist Convention from a foreign missionary society into the world's largest Protestant denomination. This section shows how the Southern Baptist Convention works today. It will describe the work of convention boards and entities and show how the Cooperative Program supports God's mission through the church.

Part 2 explores several key biblical themes to show how the mission of God determines the mission of the church. It will show that cooperation among churches is a key component of God's mission. We worship one God, a missionary God. His mission is to redeem for himself a people, the church. He has commissioned his church to make disciples of all nations by starting local churches to share in this one mission. The mission of the church, therefore, is a corporate mission, and cooperation is a means of obeying the Great Commission. It is my hope that everyone who studies these pages will be convinced that the Southern Baptist cooperative structure is more than a denominational identity; it enables Southern Baptist churches to fully participate in God's mission.

The final section makes several observations about the current state of Southern Baptist cooperation and encourages Southern Baptists, especially younger Southern Baptists, to embrace the cooperative efforts of the convention. No one operates under the illusion that everything is perfect. However, the Cooperative Program and

---

[5] Statistical data in this book has been compiled by the SBC Executive Committee based on SBC Annuals and the convention's Annual Church Profile.

[6] Tom Elliff, "First Person: Will Southern Baptists Rise to the Challenge?" Baptist Press, October 8, 2012, http://bpnews.net/38880/first-person-will-southern-baptists-rise-to-the-challenge.

[7] Leon McBeth, "Cooperation and Crisis as Shapers of Southern Baptist Identity," *Baptist History and Heritage* (1995): 35.

the cooperative structure of the convention provide means for any church, no matter its size or location, to participate in the mission of God.

I am a lifelong Southern Baptist. Through the "cradle roll" program, my name was on the roll of a Southern Baptist church months before I was born. I am a product of the Southern Baptist Convention. I was saved, mentored, and called to ministry in a Southern Baptist church. I received my education through Southern Baptist schools. I have been honored to serve on the staff of several Southern Baptist churches and as part of the administration and faculty of a Southern Baptist seminary. My passion for missions and my missionary experience are results of the Southern Baptist Convention's work. The greatest commandment is to love God with all my heart, soul, mind, and strength. Southern Baptists have helped me to love God in all of these areas. The Lord has used this convention to make me who I am.

This book is written by a Southern Baptist for Southern Baptists. It is my offering to the convention I love, as well as my plea to fellow Southern Baptists. Many predict the demise of denominations in general and the Southern Baptist Convention in particular. I refuse to believe that such demise is inevitable. My prayer is that this book will provide you with reasons to embrace the cooperative identity of this convention and work to make it the best it can be for the glory of God and the benefit of the nations.

This book is the result of my doctoral studies at Southeastern Baptist Theological Seminary. It is an attempt to transition my research and writing from the academy to the church. To be frank, the process has been more difficult than I originally imagined. A dissertation is a strange piece of literature in that it only needs to pass the inspection of a few people. I am writing this book for a larger audience. Though I have tried to eliminate technicalities and assumptions, I fear I have, in some instances, failed. This fault is mine alone. I am extremely grateful to my friend and colleague Greg Mathias. He has read every word, and provided helpful insights and corrections. I also appreciate the partnership with B&H Academic in producing this book. Thanks for reading. It is my sincere prayer that you and I will experience the fullness of Christ as we engage in God's mission together.

PART I

THE HISTORICAL DEVELOPMENT OF THE SOUTHERN BAPTIST CONVENTION

1

FROM MISSIONARY SOCIETY TO A CONVENTION OF CHURCHES

Southern Baptists have a rich history, a robust denominational structure, and a resilient identity that encourages voluntary cooperation among churches on a broad range of convention activities. The convention we see today stems from a loosely structured mission society. In 1845, a portion of that society adopted a structure that allowed for a diverse range of ministries and encouraged cooperation among local churches as the means of accomplishing this vision.[1]

AMERICAN BAPTISTS UNITE AROUND GLOBAL MISSIONS

At the beginning of the nineteenth century, Baptists in the United States had little structure beyond the local church. Some churches gathered in local associations; however, this simple structure did not translate into national, or even statewide, denominational organization. This changed on May 18, 1814, with the establishment of the General Convention of the Baptist Denomination in the United States for Foreign Missions, commonly referred to as the Triennial Convention. This convention was formed when Baptists organized themselves around the cause of foreign missions for "diffusing evangelistic light, through benighted regions of the earth."[2] The first national identity for Baptists was a missionary identity.

---

[1] This claim that the Southern Baptist Convention was established for missionary purposes is in no way an attempt to neglect what historian Leon McBeth has labeled the "blunt historical fact" that slavery was a chief issue leading to the breakup of the Triennial Convention and the founding of the Southern Baptist Convention. Leon McBeth, *Baptist Heritage* (Nashville: Broadman Press, 1987), 382.

[2] Adapted from *The Proceedings of the Baptist Convention for Missionary Purposes* (Philadelphia: Ann Coles, 1814), 6.

The story of this missionary identity for American Baptists began, ironically, with the appointment of several Congregationalist missionaries by the American Board of Commissioners of Foreign Missions. In February 1812, Adoniram and Ann Judson, along with Samuel and Harriett Newell, Samuel Nott, Gordon Hall, and Luther Rice, left the United States for a seven-month journey to India, where they planned to serve as missionaries. Adoniram Judson knew that when the group arrived, they would encounter William Carey and his team of Baptist missionaries. Judson wanted to be prepared to discuss (or perhaps refute) the Baptist beliefs about baptism, so he studied the biblical teachings on the topic. This exercise did not end as he anticipated. Judson was looking for support of the Congregationalist belief in infant baptism, but he ended up rejecting his previously held belief and accepting Baptist teaching on the subject.

Judson became convinced that the word translated *baptize* in the New Testament could only mean to immerse in water and could not be used to support any other mode of baptism. This discovery led him to question other aspects of his previously held beliefs. Further research led Judson to conclude that Christian baptism could only be understood as the immersion of professing believers. As one might imagine, this discovery was troubling. Not only did it challenge his theology; it also meant that Judson himself had never been baptized! Ann was originally opposed to Adoniram's conversion. However, after her own study of the Scriptures, she became convinced and joined him. Once they arrived in India, both Ann and Adoniram were baptized and resigned their appointment with the Congregational mission agency.

Fellow missionary Luther Rice seems to have held similar doubts about infant baptism. After talking to William Carey and reading Judson's baptism testimony, he too became a Baptist and resigned his missionary appointment. Because of their conversions, Rice and the Judsons were essentially stranded in India. They had a strong missionary calling and were firmly convinced of their new faith; however, they had no avenue for the financial support of their work. Eventually, Rice returned to the United States to raise support for the new Baptist missionary efforts. His fund-raising efforts and tireless work gave birth to the Triennial Convention. According to Baptist historian William Wright Barnes, Luther Rice, "more than any other man, may be called the organizer of the Baptist denomination in America."[3] Even though Rice originally planned to return to the mission field, he never did. Instead, he spent the rest of his life working within the Triennial Convention, providing an identity and purpose for this growing body of Christians in the new world.

In the beginning, the Triennial Convention served as a centralizing network for previously disconnected Baptist missionary societies (and individuals) scattered throughout the United States. Rice's intention for the first meeting of the Trien-

---

[3] William Wright Barnes, *The Southern Baptist Convention: A Study in the Development of Ecclesiology* (Seminary Hill, TX, 1934), 21.

nial Convention was to bring together delegates "for the purpose of forming some general combination of concert of action among them."[4] The Triennial Convention became the first ever national organization of Baptists in America. David Dockery, former president of Union University, has called this event "one of the most significant events in Baptist history."[5] However, despite the monumental nature of this organization, within thirty years the unity of the Triennial Convention was shattered and the Southern Baptist Convention formed.

Several factors contributed to the eventual breakup of the Triennial Convention. Chief among them was slave ownership and missionary appointment, which became a significant point of tension between Northern and Southern Baptists by the 1840s. As Southern Baptists saw it, barring slaveholders from missionary service precluded them from fulfilling the Great Commission and demanded the formation of a new denominational body.[6] According to Jesse Fletcher, "The Southern Baptist Convention walked on the stage of history burdened by its defense of a practice which subsequent history would condemn and which Southern Baptists themselves would one day condemn."[7]

There also seems to have been tension among Baptists about the deployment and support of home missionaries. The Southern states felt their region was underrepresented and that funds and missionaries were being directed elsewhere. However, the problems within the Triennial Convention, and its eventual breakup, can be found in the different visions for ministry and convention structure. According to Baptist historian Leon McBeth, "Whoever fails to grasp the differences between society and convention methods will never understand Northern and Southern Baptists."[8]

---

[4] Ibid. The constitution of the Triennial Convention stated that the convention should consist of "delegates, not exceeding two in number from each of several Missionary Societies, and other bodies of the Baptist Denomination, now existing, or which may hereafter be formed in the United States, and which shall regularly contribute to the general Missionary fund, a sum amounting at least to one hundred dollars per annum."

[5] David Dockery, *Southern Baptist Consensus and Renewal: A Biblical, Historical, and Theological Proposal* (Nashville: B&H Academic, 2008), 38.

[6] In the opening resolution of the 1845 convention, Southern Baptists wrote, "Were we asked to characterize the conduct of our Northern brethren in one short phrase, we should adopt that of the Apostle. It was 'Forbidding us to speak unto the Gentiles.' Did this deny us no privilege? Did it not obstruct us, lay a kind of Romish interdict upon us in the discharge of an imperative duty; a duty to which the church has been, after the lapse of ages, awakened universally and successfully; a duty the very object, of our long cherished connection and confederation?" *Proceedings of the Southern Baptist Convention Held in Augusta, Georgia, May 8th, 9th, 10th, 11th and 12th, 1845* (Richmond: H. K. Ellyson, 1845), 18.

[7] Jesse Fletcher, *The Southern Baptist Convention: A Sesquicentennial History* (Nashville: Broadman & Holman, 1994), 40.
In 1995, the messengers to the 150-year anniversary of the Southern Baptist Convention passed a resolution confessing and repenting for racism and the support of slavery in its past. The resolution openly acknowledged: "Our relationship to African-Americans has been hindered from the beginning by the role that slavery played in the formation of the Southern Baptist Convention; and . . . many of our Southern Baptist forbears defended the right to own slaves, and either participated in, supported, or acquiesced in the particularly inhumane nature of American slavery." See Southern Baptist Convention, "Resolution on Racial Reconciliation on the 150th Anniversary of the Southern Baptist Convention," SBC website, 1995, http://www.sbc.net/resolutions/amresolution.asp?id=899.

[8] McBeth, *Baptist Heritage*, 347.

Baptists in the North preferred the society model while Baptists in the South preferred a convention or associational structure.

SOCIETY VERSUS CONVENTION STRUCTURE

Convention or *association* refers to a denominational structure that is church-based and embraces a broad range of ministries. Local churches are able to support and participate in foreign and home missions, education, publishing, and other ministries by participating in one convention. The work of the convention is carried out through delegates who represent the churches of which they are members. The vision and mission of the convention are defined by the work of the whole denomination.

Societies, on the other hand, are single-cause-based. They are established and held together to serve a single ministry or purpose. Membership consists of individuals who are interested in the cause and invest financially. The society is not connected directly to the local church. Instead, individual members from churches participate or do not participate depending on their interests in the specific cause. Rather than embracing multiple causes, a society focuses on foreign missions or local missions, education or publication, or another social ministry. Each society is autonomous and is generally controlled by a board of directors who are also financial contributors to the cause.

As observed earlier, despite its name, the Triennial Convention initially operated as a society, convening individuals and other societies, rather than delegates from local churches, as a means of advancing a foreign missionary cause. However, many of the founders envisioned a Baptist denomination with a broader range of ministries. Richard Furman, the convention's first president, pled with delegates to expand the ministry beyond the foreign mission field. He wanted the convention to adopt a home mission strategy and educate pastors. In his presidential address, he said, "It is deeply to be regretted that no more attention is paid to the improvement of the minds of pious youths who are called to the gospel ministry."[9] Luther Rice shared this desire for a more expanded focus. Under their leadership, the Triennial Convention started to be involved in home missions, Christian education, and also published material for its members. However, this broader convention structure lasted less than a decade.

Most historians agree that Baptists in the North, especially New England Baptists, were unhappy the Triennial Convention had expanded its ministry beyond foreign missions, embracing a more denominational structure. Their frustration was rooted in at least two concerns. First, they expressed theological concerns. They felt the independence of the local church was being violated. Francis Wayland, pastor of

---

[9] Richard Furman, "Address," *Proceedings*, Baptist Convention for Missionary Purposes, 42. Taken from McBeth, *Baptist Heritage*, 352.

First Baptist Church in Providence, Rhode Island, said, "I do not see how a church can be *represented*." These brethren believed external organizations were made up of individuals and could not claim to work on behalf of a local church. Second, they raised practical concerns. They believed that the emphasis on other ministries diverted monies away from foreign missions. One observer, Baron Stow, claimed no new missionaries were sent to Burma between 1820 and 1823 and plans for beginning work in Brazil and Africa in 1815 were postponed because of insufficient funding.[10]

In 1826, the Triennial Convention reversed course and embraced its identity as a foreign missionary society. All other ministries were eliminated. Wayland, who originally supported a broader ministry structure, led the convention to adopt this new vision, noting the expanded ministry was viewed negatively "by so decided a majority that the attempt was never repeated, and this danger was averted. We look back at the present day, with astonishment that such an idea was ever entertained."[11]

Two other factors contributed to the redirection of the convention. First, Richard Furman died in 1825, and with his death, Baptists in the South lost one of the strongest proponents for a broader convention structure. Second, and perhaps more important, New England Baptists were able to move the 1826 convention meeting from Washington, DC, to New York. In previous meetings, they had not been able to garner enough voting support to address their concerns. In New York, however, because of the expense and difficulty of travel from the South, the largest voting bloc was made up of delegates from the Northern states. Of the 63 delegates, 23 were from Massachusetts and 17 were from New York. This coalition made the way for a change in convention structure and leadership. The society method won the day within the Triennial Convention, and regional tensions flared, a factor that eventually contributed to the establishment of the Southern Baptist Convention.

SOUTHERN BAPTISTS CHOOSE A CONVENTION

According to historian Robert A. Torbet, when Baptists from the southern United States gathered in 1845, they chose a "new type of Baptist organization."[12] McBeth observed that Baptists in the South "favored a unified, cooperative denomination in which one general convention did various forms of ministry" while Baptists in the North "preferred an independent society approach."[13] It is important to understand why Baptists in the South preferred (or did not oppose) the associational method

---

[10] McBeth, *Baptist Heritage*, 357–58.

[11] Francis Wayland, *Notes on the Principles and Practices of Baptist Churches* (Boston: Gould and Lincoln, 1856), 184, cited in Robert Andrew Baker, *The Southern Baptist Convention and Its People: 1607–1972* (Nashville: Broadman Press, 1974), 112.

[12] Robert A. Torbet, *A History of the Baptists* (Valley Forge, PA: Judson Press, 2000), 293.

[13] Leon McBeth, "The Broken Unity of 1845: A Reassessment," *Baptist Heritage* (July 1998): 28.

for missions and ministry support. They shared similar convictions regarding the autonomy and independence of the local church. But where Baptists in the North rejected associationalism, Baptists in the South embraced it. Multiple factors contributed to this.

First, the social structure of Southern communities encouraged associationalism. New England states were made up of townships. These townships were governed through strict democratic rule; each citizen attended town meetings expecting to have a voice and a vote in local decisions. This fostered a sense of individual responsibility in decision making. Southern states, on the other hand, governed themselves quite differently. Rather than townships, these communities were made up of counties. McBeth observed that the social structure of Southern counties was "at times almost feudal."[14] Decision making was not the exclusive responsibility of the masses but was more centralized. This form of government seems to have made Baptists in the South more comfortable with a representative denominational structure.

Second, William Wright Barnes has noted that another reason Baptists in the South were more willing to embrace associationalism can be found in their statements of faith. These statements allowed, if not encouraged, formal cooperation between local churches. For most Baptist churches in the South, the statement of faith developed by the Philadelphia Association served as the primary confession. This document affirmed the existence of both the universal and the local church. While it described local churches as having autonomy and the authority to carry out all ministries, discipline, and the establishing of leadership, the confession also noted that God's command for believers was to "walk together in particular societies, or churches, for their mutual edification." The Philadelphia Confession does not seem to acknowledge any conflict between cooperation and local church authority. Even the South's General Baptists, most of whom settled in Virginia and North Carolina, though opposed to aspects of the Calvinistic theology espoused by the Philadelphia Association, adopted confessions that encouraged partnership between churches. Barnes noted, "Although [they] were Arminian in theology . . . they held to a centralized ecclesiology in agreement with the fundamental spiritual idea of Philadelphia."[15] Whereas early Southern Baptists held different understandings about nuanced aspects of the doctrine of salvation, they held enough agreement on the doctrine of the church to make space for voluntary association between churches.

Third, many Baptists in the South had already experienced the benefits of cooperation and realized that voluntary association did not necessarily undermine local church autonomy. One of the largest and most influential associations was the Sandy Creek Association. Philadelphia pastor Morgan Edwards observed that in just 17 years, this association had "spread branches westward as far as the great river

---

[14] McBeth, *Baptist Heritage*, 350.
[15] Barnes, *The Southern Baptist Convention*, 7.

Mississippi; southward as far a Georgia; eastward to the sea and Chesopeek bay [*sic*] and Northward to the waters of Potowmack [*sic*]."[16] The Sandy Creek Association was more than a friendly gathering. This association engaged in many functions that were typically considered the responsibility of the local church: placement and ordination of ministers, baptism, administration of ordinances, and church discipline. These churches were comfortable with associationalism, and when the Southern Baptist Convention formed, they embraced a centralized organization and cooperative ministry.

Fourth, and perhaps the most significantly, Southern Baptists chose a different structure due to the leadership and influence of two men: Richard Furman and W. B. Johnson. Richard Furman was the pastor of First Baptist Church in Charleston, South Carolina, from 1787 until his death in 1825. As noted earlier, when he served as president of the Triennial Convention, Furman was a strong advocate of a denominational structure supporting a wide range of ministries. Furman's greatest influence came through his protégé W. B. Johnson, the first president of the Southern Baptist Convention.

Johnson was arguably the most influential person with regard to the structure of the Southern Baptist Convention. Even before 1845, he was a recognized leader among Baptists. He served as a pastor in Georgia and South Carolina, and while in South Carolina, worked to organize the state convention and served as its president. Johnson also served on the organizational committee and eventually served as president of the Triennial Convention. Johnson's reputation and previous leadership experience helped him lead the SBC to adopt a structure that supported a wide range of ministries and encouraged congregational cooperation.

At the first gathering of Southern Baptists in 1845, Johnson described two possible structures for the new denomination:

> I invite your attention to the consideration of two plans: The one is that which has been adopted for years past, viz.: separate and independent bodies for the prosecution of each object. . . .
>
> The other proposes one Convention, embodying the whole Denomination, together with separate and distinct Boards, for each object of benevolent enterprise, located at different places, and all amendable to the Convention.[17]

According to McBeth, "It is clear which plan Johnson favored; in fact, in his coat pocket he already had a draft of a constitution which would set the new Southern

---

[16] Morgan Edwards, *Materials Toward a History of Baptists*, 2:92.

[17] Robert A. Baker, *A Baptist Source Book, with Particular Reference to Southern Baptists* (Nashville: Broadman Press, 1966), 114.

body on the convention plan."[18] At last, Baptists in the United States seemed to have become what Luther Rice and Richard Furman hoped the Triennial Convention could be.

From the first meeting in 1845, Southern Baptists chose a structure that was quite different from the one they were leaving. Article V of the new constitution stated, "The Convention shall elect . . . as many Boards of Managers, as in its judgment will be necessary for carrying out the benevolent objects it may determine to promote."[19] Jesse Fletcher noted, "These brief words ensured that Johnson's Furman-nurtured concept of a broad-based denomination effort . . . was in place."[20] At the inaugural meeting in Augusta, Southern Baptists established the Foreign Mission Board and the Domestic Mission Board. In 1859, Southern Baptists opened the first denominational school for training pastors and missionaries, the Southern Baptist Theological Seminary. Then, in 1891, Southern Baptists established a Sunday School Board, charged with printing denominational literature for churches. Within relatively few years, Southern Baptists had taken strides to establish a convention with a wide range of ministries.

[18] McBeth, *Baptist Heritage*, 389.
[19] See "Original Constitution of the Southern Baptist Convention," 3, at Baptist Studies Online, accessed June 7, 2017, http://baptiststudiesonline.com/wp-content/uploads/2007/02/constitution-of-the-sbc.pdf.
[20] Fletcher, *The Southern Baptist Convention*, 49.

2

THE SBC ADOPTS A COOPERATIVE IDENTITY

The decision by Southern Baptists to create a convention with a broad ministry vision and a centralized structure was the first step toward becoming the cooperative convention we are familiar with today. The SBC established a different structure and organization for directing denominational activities, yet funding mechanics remained problematic for years to come. In the beginning, each mission board was responsible for maintaining its own budget and raising its own support. The convention provided guidance and oversight, but there was no unifying financial plan. In 1846, the convention approved a request from the Board of Home Missions to hire agents who were charged with "the duty of not only collecting the funds for the society, but, especially with the promotion of religious and missionary zeal among the ministries and the churches."[1] Eventually both mission boards used agents for promoting their respective work.

Results of the agents' work were mixed. Reverend S. A. Creath of the Foreign Mission Board spent a portion of March 1859 in an Alabama association and reported raising more than $400.00 despite being "much hindered by frequent rains and high water."[2] In the same month the year before, with no agent working in the area, the same association sent only $4.00 to the board. Reverend M. Ball reported that in 1857, he rode part of the year through the Chickasaw Association of Mississippi and raised $540.00. The next year, with no agent working in the association, it raised less than $100.00.[3] Despite these positive reports, in 1859, the Board of Domestic and

---

[1] See "Editorial," *Ford's Christian Repository and Home Circle* 68, no. 1 (July 1889): 314.
[2] *Proceedings of the Seventh Biennial Session of the Southern Baptist Convention, Held in the First Baptist Church, Richmond, Virginia, May 6th, 7th, 8th, 9th and 10th, 1859* (Richmond: H. K. Ellyson's Steam Presses), 57, available online at Baylor Digital Collections, http://digitalcollections.baylor.edu/cdm/ref/collection/ml-sbcann/id/8179.
[3] Ibid.

Indian Missions,[4] while acknowledging the benefit of soliciting agents, asked if there was perhaps a better plan. In their report, they noted that fund-raising strategies were agitating and annoying to the convention and were also "rather unprofitable to the general cause."[5] Over time, churches began to complain about the aggressiveness and frequency of special offerings.

Not only were the churches frustrated by the fund-raising agents; this method was also not cost-effective. The Home Mission Board reported in 1876, "There is a marked disproportion between the receipts of the Board and the amount paid for salaries and traveling expenses of Secretaries and agents . . . costing nearly 44 per cent of the whole collection. And the costs of the collection agents are over 53 per cent of what is received through them."[6] This report was followed by an impassioned appeal for "radical changes in our methods of securing contributions." Through the years there arose a growing concern and deep-seated conviction that the convention needed a better way to support its work.

In 1913, delegates to the Southern Baptist Convention voted to establish a group to study a better way to finance the work of the convention. This group came to be known as the "Efficiency Committee" because it was tasked to find "the highest efficiency of our forces and the fullest possible enlistment of our people for the work of the Kingdom in the critical and strategic time in which we live and serve."[7] The following year, the committee presented a report and asked all convention boards to operate in a more cooperative fashion and avoid any appearance of competition. It also proposed an end to general fund-raising programs without consultation and permission from the whole convention. Perhaps the most important recommendation was for the convention to develop a unified budget that would support all of the convention's work. According to the committee's plan, this budget could include the work of state conventions and associations.[8] Even though it would take another thirty years before the Southern Baptist Convention implemented something like these recommendations, the proposals of the Efficiency Committee demonstrate that Southern Baptists rejected the society method and were searching for some-

---

[4] Throughout Southern Baptist history, the name of the board responsible for domestic missionary work was known by different names. For historical accuracy, I will use the name by which it is referred in the specific document being referenced.

[5] *Proceedings of the Seventh Biennial Session of the Southern Baptist Convention*, 57.

[6] See *Proceedings of the Twenty-First Session of the Southern Baptist Convention, Held with the First Baptist Church, in Richmond, VA, May 11, 12, 13, 15, 1876* (Richmond: Dispatch Steam Printing House, 1876), 27, available online from Baylor Digital Collections, http://digitalcollections.baylor.edu/cdm/ref/collection/ml-sbcann/id/185.

[7] See *Annual of the Southern Baptist Convention, 1913*, held in St. Louis, MO (Nashville: Marshall & Bruce, 1913), 70, available online at Baylor Digital Collections, http://digitalcollections.baylor.edu/cdm/ref/collection/ml-sbcann/id/3040.

[8] *Annual of the Southern Baptist Convention, 1914* (Nashville: Marshall & Bruce, 1914), 70–78, available online at Baylor Digital Collections, http://digitalcollections.baylor.edu/cdm/ref/collection/ml-sbcann/id/4243.

thing new. The work of the convention should depend less on fund-raising agents, they believed, and more on a cooperative body with a unified vision and budget.

THE SEVENTY-FIVE MILLION CAMPAIGN: A WATERSHED MOMENT IN THE SHAPING OF SOUTHERN BAPTIST IDENTITY

In 1919, Rosco Owen Fleming raised money to erect a monument in the center of Enterprise, Alabama. The monument stands as one of the most unusual tributes in the United States. It is a monument to an insect—the boll weevil.[9] This insect invaded the United States in the early 1900s. In 1916 it destroyed the cotton crops in Alabama, causing the economy to collapse. The crop failure forced farmers to consider new sources of income: peanuts, sweet potatoes, soybeans, and eventually chickens. As a result of this creative thinking, the Alabama economy rebounded, and in 1917, farmers produced the largest peanut harvest in the United States. The creativity and diversification triggered by this disaster actually stabilized the region against later natural disasters.

The plaque under the boll weevil statue reads:

> In profound appreciation of the Boll Weevil and what it has done as the Herald of Prosperity, this monument was erected by the Citizens of Enterprise, Coffee County, Alabama.

The same year the monument to the boll weevil was unveiled in Enterprise, Alabama, Southern Baptists launched the Seventy-Five Million Campaign. This event was a watershed in Southern Baptist history. Like the boll weevil, at first glance, the campaign appears to have been a disaster: the goal and pledges were not met, convention boards and agencies incurred huge debts, and the convention stood on the verge of bankruptcy. However, also like the boll weevil crisis, the campaign and the subsequent recovery efforts forced Southern Baptists to think creatively. The Seventy-Five Million Campaign served as the launching pad for development of an identity and structure in which cooperation became a central virtue for Southern Baptists. This virtue remains one of the key reasons for the success and expanse of the Southern Baptist Convention.

Six months after the end of World War I, Southern Baptists met in Atlanta, Georgia, for the seventy-fourth meeting of the Southern Baptist Convention. In his opening address, SBC president J. B. Gambrell pointed out that the war's devastation created a global opportunity for Southern Baptists. He said, "The attentive

---

[9] Ben Berntson, "Boll Weevil Monument," *Encyclopedia of Alabama*, accessed July 30, 2014, http://www.encyclopediaofalabama.org/face/Article.jsp?id=h-2384; and Dan Fesperman, "'Bug' Monument Is a Complex Topic: The Boll Weevil Monument in Enterprise, Ala., Honors the Insect That Forced the Area to Diversify," *Seattle Times*, April 1, 1999.

ear can hear from every part of the world voices calling us 'Come over and help us.'"[10] Later in the meeting, a "committee on financial aspect of enlarged program" reported, "In view of the needs of the world at this hour, in view of the numbers and ability of Southern Baptists, we suggest . . . that in the organized work of this convention we undertake to raise not less than $75,000,000 in the next five years."[11] This figure was probably set as a way of honoring the seventy-fifth anniversary of the convention. The delegates accepted the challenge, and November 30–December 7, 1919, was designated "Victory Week." This was the week all Southern Baptist churches were to report all their pledges to the convention. Southern Baptists spent the following months organizing and securing commitments. In the end, they pledged $92,630,923, exceeding the goal by more than 20 percent.

However, the exuberance soon faded. The financial collapse that followed the war devastated the Southern economy. By the end of the campaign, giving fell well short of the pledged amount. In fact, giving fell short of the goal by more than $16,000,000, with actual receipts totaling $58,591,713.96. It is no understatement to claim that this failed fund-raising effort has shaped Southern Baptist identity even into our day. The Seventy-Five Million Campaign changed the Southern Baptist Convention financially, structurally, and theologically.

Failure to meet pledges created more than a sense of embarrassment; the financial shortfall became a full-scale financial crisis. Boards and agencies budgeted, took out loans, and even spent based on the pledged amounts. By 1926, at the end of the campaign, the Southern Baptist Convention had a staggering debt for the time of approximately $6,500,000. This financial crisis was compounded by the debts incurred by various state conventions. SBC leaders worked with creditors to restructure loans, but despite their best efforts, in 1926 the Southern Baptist Convention quite literally stood on the brink of financial ruin.

SOUTHERN BAPTISTS EMBRACE COOPERATION AS THE WAY FORWARD

Despite the financial problems created by the Seventy-Five Million Campaign, it was not a complete failure. In 1921, the SBC received a report that:

> He [God] has wonderfully unified, solidified, organized, informed, and inspired our people[:] The tides of spiritual and evangelistic and missionary power which have swept over our churches, bringing hundreds of thousands into the fold . . . the deepening of the prayer life of our churches, the calling out of more than 10,000 of our young people

---

[10] *Annual of the Southern Baptist Convention 1919* (Nashville: Marshall & Bruce, 1919), 17, available online at Baylor Digital Collections, http://digitalcollections.baylor.edu/cdm/ref/collection/ml-sbcann/id/6706.
[11] Ibid., 74.

in the spirit of voluntary service to give their lives to Him, the development of a great denominational consciousness ...[12]

This spiritual renewal and numerical growth was accompanied by an increased awareness of Southern Baptist potential. Before 1919 few churches had a plan for encouraging financial commitments or regular giving of members. In the months leading up to Victory Week, campaign leaders and pastors worked feverishly to elicit pledges from as many church members as possible. These efforts coincided with an increase in per capita giving among Southern Baptist churches of more than 100 percent between 1914 and 1929.

Years	Avg. Annual Per Capita Contribution
1914–1918	$5.08
1919–1924	$9.37
1925–1929	$10.52

According to Fred Grissom, "Many Baptists saw for the first time what could be accomplished by establishing budgets, conducting every-member canvasses, and practicing weekly giving. In a real sense, the campaign itself, including its failures, was the most effective training in stewardship most Baptists had ever had."[13] By joining together in a cooperative effort, Southern Baptists raised more money and involved more churches than ever before in the history of the convention.

The Cooperative Program (CP)

The Seventy-Five Million Campaign taught Southern Baptists the power of cooperation, a unified budget, and a denominational stewardship plan. The financial crisis facing the Southern Baptist Convention and the lessons learned throughout the Seventy-Five Million Campaign served as motivation for Southern Baptists to more fully embrace what Baptist historian Robert Baker called "the genius of the convention-type program."[14] Southern Baptists developed a formal system of cooperation between local churches, state conventions, and the national convention. At the 1925 SBC meeting in Memphis, Tennessee, delegates adopted a motion to establish the Cooperative Program, a plan for financing all the activities of the

---

[12] *Annual of the Southern Baptist Convention 1921* (Nashville: Marshall & Bruce, 1921), 33, available online at Baylor Digital Collections, http://digitalcollections.baylor.edu/cdm/ref/collection/ml-sbcann/id/16881.

[13] Fred Grissom, "Cooperation through Stewardship," *Baptist History and Heritage* (January 1989): 27.

[14] Baker, *The Southern Baptist Convention and Its People*, 404 (see chap. 1, n. 11).

convention through one general budget. This program became (and remains) the primary funding mechanism for all convention activities.

Through the years, Southern Baptists have sought to improve the functionality of the Cooperative Program. They have made adjustments in how funds are distributed and in the mechanisms of accounting and promotion; however, the Cooperative Program remains the financial driving force for much of the expanse and success of the convention. One unified budget, and the expectation of regular contributions, allows boards to plan their work without being encumbered by the constant need to engage in fund-raising or pay agents in the field.

However, the importance of the Cooperative Program should not be reduced to its funding capacity. In many ways, the Cooperative Program is responsible for forming and even galvanizing Southern Baptist identity. McBeth argued that the Cooperative Program illustrates "a near canonization of the word [cooperation] and the concept among Southern Baptists. . . . To be 'non-cooperative, is a serious thing to Southern Baptists, and to be 'independent' has become a severe criticism."[15] Southern Baptist churches are judged, and convention leaders are evaluated, based on their support of the Cooperative Program and cooperation throughout convention ministries. For many, cooperation is more than mere allegiance to convention causes. To cooperate is to be Southern Baptist. For many, lack of cooperation is not simply denominational treason; it is viewed as a spiritual defect.

The Baptist Faith and Message and the Doctrine of Cooperation

A second, but often overlooked, impact of the Seventy-Five Million Campaign is how it set the stage for the doctrine of cooperation to be included in the 1925 Baptist Faith and Message, the official statement of faith for the Southern Baptist Convention. This statement was taken almost verbatim from the 1833 New Hampshire Confession. However, one of the most notable changes was the addition of a statement including cooperation as a Christian doctrine. Historians have argued this addition grew out of denominational conflicts stemming from the Seventy-Five Million Campaign. The decision of Southern Baptists to develop a theological statement on cooperation served as a signal that they were forming a unique denominational identity.

As noted earlier, the success of the Seventy-Five Million Campaign was severely impacted by the postwar economic recession. However, economic struggles were not the only forces fighting against the campaign. The modernist/fundamentalist controversy, which swept through the United States during those same years, also influenced the campaign. Baptist historian Andrew Smith has noted that this theo-

---

[15] McBeth, *Baptist Heritage*, 622.

logical controversy "drove a wedge between Northern and Southern Baptists and caused Southern Baptist leaders to begin to see their denomination as something other than a regional branch of a wider tradition."[16] As Southern Baptists responded to this theological battle, they developed a distinct identity and began to view themselves as something more than Baptists who happen to live in the South.

George Marsden, in his monumental work *Understanding Fundamentalism and Evangelicalism,* reported that after the First World War, the social fabric of the United States changed significantly.[17] Urbanization and immigration introduced new ideas and lifestyles into a culture that previously viewed itself as exclusively Protestant. These social shifts were accompanied by the introduction of Protestant liberalism, the Social Gospel, and German higher criticism. These religious movements deemphasized the supernatural, denied the historicity of much of the Scripture, and elevated ethics over personal conversion. Though some Christian leaders embraced these changes as modern progress, another group considered them a direct assault on the Christian faith. The concerns of the latter group gave birth to the theological movement known as *Fundamentalism.*

Concerns over the theological changes in America were addressed in a twelve-volume set of essays, later edited into a four-book set, called *The Fundamentals.* In 1920, Curtis Lee Law, editor of the *Watchman-Examiner,* coined the term *Fundamentalism* as a label for the school of thought that defended the ideas presented in these books. In time, Fundamentalists developed a set of theological affirmations that came to be known as the "five points of fundamentalism": (1) the inerrancy of Scripture; (2) the deity of Christ, including affirmation of his virgin birth; (3) the substitutionary atonement of Christ's death; (4) the physical/bodily resurrection of Christ; and (5) the miracle working power of Christ.[18] Along with these theological affirmations, Fundamentalists also tended to embrace a militant attitude. Their passion was fueled by the notion that their movement was the only hope for the future of Christianity. In their estimation, a person (or church) had either embraced Fundamentalism or Liberalism; there was no middle ground.

Though most Southern Baptists shared the same theological concerns as Fundamentalists, they possessed strong denominational loyalty and were hesitant to embrace Fundamentalism because of its militant and divisive character. The tendency of Fundamentalists to disrupt meetings by engaging in public debate and to create division within denominations was believed to be undignified and unnecessary by some Southern Baptists.[19] Smith wrote, "While Fundamentalism was a centripetal

---

[16] Andrew C. Smith, "Flocking Themselves Together: Fundamentalism, Fundraising, and the Bureaucratization of the Southern Baptist Convention 1919–1925" (PhD diss., Vanderbilt University, 2011), 174.

[17] George Marsden, *Understanding Fundamentalism and Evangelicalism* (Grand Rapids: Eerdmans, 1991), 13–14.

[18] This list was first promoted at the Niagara Bible Conference in 1910.

[19] Smith, "Flocking Themselves Together," 99–103.

force that tore at the unity of Northern Protestants, it became for Southern Baptists a catalyst for organizational development and an ingredient in the content that held their denomination together."[20] The theological debate, coupled with the offensive behavior of some Fundamentalists, seem to have been key factors that caused Southern Baptists to embrace cooperation as a denominational priority.

To better understand how pressure from Fundamentalism helped birth the cooperative identity of the Southern Baptist Convention, we need to look no further than a series of public conflicts about the Seventy-Five Million Campaign between J. Frank Norris and L. R. Scarborough, two influential Texas Baptists. Norris was one of the most influential pastors in the United States. He is credited with bringing Fundamentalism to the South. According to Barry Hankins, "During his lifetime he was one of the most hated men in Southern Baptist circles and one of the most admired among fundamentalists."[21] Scarborough, on the other hand, was a Southern Baptist statesman. He served as president of Southwestern Baptist Theological Seminary, as president of the Southern Baptist Convention, and on the Executive Committee of the Baptist General Convention of Texas. He also served as an influential member of the committee charged with writing the Baptist Faith and Message. Norris and Scarborough had different visions for the Southern Baptist Convention, and one of the central points of conflict was the Seventy-Five Million Campaign.

Scarborough was chosen as general director of the Seventy-Five Million Campaign and believed it was a beneficial program for denominational advancement and mission. Norris violently disagreed. Allyn Russell claims Norris "despised [the Seventy-Five Million Campaign] . . . as dictatorial, unscriptural, [and] a foolish waste of hard-earned mission money."[22] According to Barry Hankins, "Norris rebelled against the campaign in the name of Baptist principle, the autonomy of the local church."[23] As Norris saw it, Fundamentalism was cut from the same cloth as the Protestant Reformation. It was a rebellion against the established, heretical church or denomination. He despised the Seventy-Five Million Campaign because he saw it as a means for increasing denominational intrusion into local church ministry. Such hierarchy was a threat to local church independence. Scarborough, on the other hand, saw Fundamentalism as a serious threat to the future health of the convention and, more important at that time, a direct threat to the success of the Seventy-Five Million Campaign.

In response to Norris's criticisms, Scarborough wrote several articles in Baptist newspapers. Over time, as he fought against Norris's rhetoric, he began to develop

[20] Ibid.
[21] Barry Hankins, *God's Rascal: J. Frank Norris and the Beginning of Southern Fundamentalism* (Lexington: University of Kentucky Press, 1996), 19.
[22] Allyn Russell, *Voices of Fundamentalism: Seven Biographical Studies* (Philadelphia, PA: Westminster Press, 1976), 37.
[23] Hankins, *God's Rascal*, 27.

the idea that cooperation was a Christian doctrine. In 1921 he wrote, "This doctrine of co-operation is a fundamental doctrine. The progress of doctrines depends on the doctrine of co-operation; disloyalty to this doctrine of co-operation is the most vicious and menacing disloyalty in the program of Jesus Christ."[24] This was a direct attack against Norris and his Fundamentalist brethren, who celebrated independence and separation as spiritual virtues. Scarborough argued that failure to cooperate, or intentionally working against cooperation, was more than a failure to support the denomination. It was disobedience to a basic biblical doctrine. The Fundamentalists' lack of cooperation was placed in the same category as denial of the truthfulness of Scripture. In this way, Scarborough argued Fundamentalists were guilty of the same type of error as their opponents, the Modernists.

In 1924, Southern Baptists appointed a committee, including Scarborough, to explore the benefits of putting together an official statement of faith. The primary reason Southern Baptists wanted an official document was to address the teaching of evolution in Baptist colleges. As noted earlier in this chapter, the committee used both the wording and the structure of the New Hampshire Confession, one of the most notable changes being the addition of a statement on cooperation:

> Christ's people should, as occasion requires, organize such associations and conventions as may best secure co-operation for the great objects of the Kingdom of God. Such organizations have no authority over each other or over the churches. They are voluntary and advisory bodies designed to elicit, combine, and direct the energies of our people in the most effective manner. Individual members of New Testament churches should co-operate with each other, and the churches themselves should co-operate with each other in carrying forward the missionary, educational, and benevolent program for the extension of Christ's Kingdom. Christian unity in the New Testament sense is spiritual harmony and voluntary co-operation for common ends by various groups of Christ's people. It is permissible and desirable as between the various Christian denominations, when the end to be attained is itself justified, and when such co-operation involves no violation of conscience or compromise of loyalty to Christ and his Word as revealed in the New Testament.[25]

The Baptist Faith and Message was designed to exclude from the convention those who were too far to the left as well as those too far to the right.

---

[24] L. R. Scarborough, "The Heresy of Non-Co-operation," *Baptist Messenger*, November 17, 1921, 4.

[25] 1925 Baptist Faith and Message Statement, Article 22, "Co-operation," in "Comparison of 1925, 1963 and 2000 Baptist Faith and Message," Southern Baptist Convention website, accessed June 7, 2017, http://www.sbc.net/bfm2000/bfmcomparison.asp.

To be fair, Southern Baptists did not (and do not) understand the doctrine of cooperation to be on par with more cardinal doctrines—Scripture, theology proper, Christology, soteriology, and so on. However, including cooperation among these cherished Christian doctrines indicates it is a key component of denominational identity. Since 1925, Southern Baptists have revised the Baptist Faith and Message twice. In each revision, the statement on cooperation has remained as a clear indication that Southern Baptists are firmly committed to cooperation as an important feature of convention structure and identity.

3

How Southern Baptists Cooperate on Mission

The previous chapter showed how Southern Baptists came to embrace cooperation as a doctrine and a denominational structure. This chapter shows how Southern Baptists practice cooperation. First, we will look at the Cooperative Program. This section will provide a brief overview of how funds flow from the local church to the different SBC entities. Next, we will look at how the Southern Baptist Convention has structured itself to accomplish God's mission. The SBC is more than 175 years old. As one can imagine, there have been many structural changes. We will not take the time to examine all of these. However, there have been two important adjustments over the past two decades: the Covenant for a New Century and the Great Commission Resurgence. Both of these affect the way the convention works today, so we will look briefly at each. Finally, the chapter will present a brief overview of the entities that represent Southern Baptist cooperation and mission.

The Cooperative Program—How It Works

The Cooperative Program is not ingenious merely because it is a single source of funding for Southern Baptist Convention activities. Almost all large organizations have a unified budget from which expenses are paid. The unique power of the Cooperative Program is that it comports with Baptists' belief in the authority of the local church while also serving as a unified channel for funding missions and ministries. The Cooperative Program, even though it funds a global organization, is a local church program. It is structured and promoted as the avenue through which local churches participate in God's global mission.

To appreciate what is meant by the preceding paragraph, it is important to understand how the Cooperative Program works. There are exceptions to every rule, but overall, what is described represents how the vast majority of Southern Baptist churches engage in missions through the Cooperative Program.

The Cooperative Program is for, and by, the local church. Each week, local churches collect voluntary offerings from those who attend their services. These funds are given in obedience to the biblical expectation for Christians to support the mission and ministry of the local church. Some churches teach that the Bible requires all Christians to give a tithe (10 percent) of their income to the church. Others reject the idea that the Bible requires a specific percentage. Rather, they claim all Christians should give what they can in response to God's grace. Regardless of what a particular church teaches, all Baptist churches believe these offerings should be given to the local church freely and without compulsion.

Each local church establishes a ministry budget, which includes funds to support Southern Baptist causes through the Cooperative Program. Typically, the local church allocates a percentage of their undesignated offerings for this purpose. The Southern Baptist Convention does not require churches to give a specified percentage. Individual churches, by whatever decision-making process they choose, decide how they will participate. In other words, it is a mistake to understand the Cooperative Program as a denominational tax, or dues to be paid for membership. All authority and decision making, from beginning to end, rests with the local church.

At some time during the month, the person (or team) in the local church responsible for financial distribution calculates and sends all Cooperative Program funds to the Baptist state convention or conventions with which their congregation cooperates. Since the inception of the Cooperative Program, individual state conventions have collected all Cooperative Program monies; the individual church sends one check or electronic payment to the state convention to support both state convention and broader Southern Baptist Convention ministries.[1] The state convention, in turn, sends an appropriated, predetermined percentage of these funds to the Executive Committee of the Southern Baptist Convention for distribution and support of Southern Baptist cooperative ministries.

One frequently asked question is, "How does the state convention decide how much money should remain in the state and how much should be sent to the Southern Baptist Convention?" The simple answer is, messengers from churches determine this during annual state convention meetings. A longer answer is: each state convention develops an annual budget according to its ministry needs. This budgeting process differs from state to state, but the result is that each state convention retains a percentage of Cooperative Program funds to support state convention ministries. Many state conventions also establish a percentage of the funds needed for promo-

---

[1] Churches may give directly to specific Southern Baptist Convention entities. However, this section describes the normal flow of funds through the Cooperative Program, for which the state convention(s) is the primary collection agent.

tion and administration of the Cooperative Program—a category known as "shared ministry expenses." The rest of the CP funds are designated for SBC causes. Each state convention's budget is then presented at the annual state convention meeting and adopted, rejected, or amended by messengers from churches.

The Executive Committee is responsible for the collection of funds received from state conventions for SBC causes. Those funds are disbursed according to a formula adopted at the Southern Baptist Convention annual meeting by messengers from churches.[2] A small percentage is kept to support basic operating expenses of the SBC, and the rest is distributed between the International Mission Board, the North American Mission Board (NAMB), six Southern Baptist seminaries, and the Ethics and Religious Liberty Commission. The 2015–2016 Cooperative Program budget allocated 50.41 percent to the International Mission Board, 22.79 percent to the North American Mission Board, 22.16 percent to Theological Education,[3] 1.65 percent to the Ethics and Religious Liberty Commission, and 2.99 percent to the Executive Committee to cover SBC operating expenses. Each year, at the annual meeting of the Southern Baptist Convention, the messengers elect trustees to serve as stewards of each SBC entity. These trustees are charged with institutional oversight, which includes development and management of the budget. The SBC is a large organization; however, the major funding mechanism, the Cooperative Program, is structured as the means by which local churches cooperate in the mission of the convention.

Before moving on to a discussion about the specific way Southern Baptists leverage cooperative giving, it is important to address a couple of questions. The flow of funds seems simple enough; however, there are some potentially confusing aspects of Cooperative Program giving.

Important Questions about Cooperative Program Giving

1. Are Southern Baptist churches required to give a certain amount through the Cooperative Program to be a part of the SBC?

No. Once a church begins cooperating with the SBC, there are only two ways to sever that relationship: Either the church can formally express its intention to cease cooperation with the convention, or the convention can withdraw fellowship from

---

[2] Most churches cooperate with both a Baptist state convention and the Southern Baptist Convention. However, each state convention is autonomous, as is the SBC. Cooperation with a state convention does not automatically cause a church also to be in cooperation with the SBC.

[3] Of this, 21.92 percent was divided among the six SBC seminaries and .24 percent was allotted to the Southern Baptist Historical Library and Archives. 2014–15 Southern Baptist Convention Cooperative Program Allocation Budget Proposal, accessed June 8, 2017, http://www.sbc.net/pdf/cp/2014-2015CPAllocationBudget.pdf.

the church. A Southern Baptist church remains a Southern Baptist church even if it fails to give through CP in a given year, or a series of years.

A separate issue is the seating of messengers from a church at the SBC annual meeting. In 2015, the constitution of the Southern Baptist Convention was adjusted to more clearly explain what a church must do to send messengers to the annual meeting in a given year. Per article III, for a church to have their messengers "seated" at the annual meeting, the church must be deemed "in friendly cooperation with the Convention, and sympathetic with its purposes and work." The constitution states that a church may receive this designation if it meets the following criteria:

> (1) Has a faith and practice which closely identifies with the Convention's adopted statement of faith. (By way of example, churches which act to affirm, approve, or endorse homosexual behavior would be deemed not to be in cooperation with the Convention.)

> (2) Has formally approved its intention to cooperate with the Southern Baptist Convention. (By way of example, the regular filing of the annual report requested by the Convention would be one indication of such cooperation.)

> (3) Has made undesignated, financial contribution(s) through the Cooperative Program, and/or through the Convention's Executive Committee for Convention causes, and/or to any Convention entity during the fiscal year preceding.[4]

Article III also states that every cooperating church may send a minimum of two messengers, with additional messengers granted based on giving to Southern Baptist causes. This article does not require a specific amount; however, it encourages that financial contributions be made through the Cooperative Program.

Before moving on, it is important to highlight that local churches give *through* not *to* the Cooperative Program. This is an important distinction. The Cooperative Program should not be viewed as a program to be supported, but rather as the conduit through which more than 46,000 Southern Baptist churches join together for the support of convention efforts.

2. Are local Baptist associations funded through the Cooperative Program?

No. Cooperative Program gifts only support state convention and Southern Baptist Convention ministries. Churches give directly to local associations. Some

---

[4] See Southern Baptist Convention Const., art. III, at http://www.sbc.net/aboutus/legal/constitution.asp.

churches give a specific amount from the annual budget while others use a set percentage.

3. Is there a standard percentage of Cooperative Program money that remains in the state and that is sent to the SBC?

No. Each state convention is free to determine this percentage. Recently, the Great Commission Task Force recommended that all state conventions strive for a 50/50 split in distribution of funds after the deduction of shared expenses for CP promotion and administration. Several conventions have taken steps to follow this recommendation; however, the Southern Baptist Convention does not have authority to mandate the percentage of CP receipts a state convention must forward to SBC causes. Currently, six state conventions forward at least half of CP receipts to SBC causes, five without deducting shared ministry expenses.[5] According to SBC records, the average state convention contribution to SBC causes is about 38 percent.[6] The percentages change from year to year and vary from convention to convention. All of this information is publicly available. Check with your state convention to better understand specifics of how they operate.

4. What happens to Cooperative Program funds that remain with each state convention?

Remember: the Cooperative Program is the means by which local churches participate in the mission of the convention. This is as true of individual state conventions as it is of the SBC. Each state convention engages in a wide range of ministry and local church support. It would be impossible to create an exhaustive list of state convention ministries. However, the list would include supporting children's homes, hospitals, and homes for senior citizens. State conventions also support Baptist colleges, universities, and Bible schools, as well as Baptist Student Ministries at hundreds of colleges and universities. Churches in crisis are frequently supported by ministries of the state convention. Many state conventions support evangelistic ministries, church revitalization ministries, and new church plants within the state. Perhaps the most visible ministry provided through state conventions is disaster relief, a ministry coordinated in many instances by the North American Mission Board. Through the various disaster relief ministries of state conventions, Southern Baptists make up the second largest disaster relief agency in the world, second only to

---

[5] Southern Baptists of Texas (55/45), Florida (51/49), Iowa (50/50), Ohio, (50/50), and Nevada (50/50) do not deduct a shared ministry expense. The Kentucky Baptist Convention does deduct the shared ministry expense. Tammi Reed Ledbetter, "WRAP-UP: Over Half States Boost CP Sending to SBC Causes," Baptist Press, December 21, 2016, http://www.bpnews.net/48089/wrapup-over-half-states-boost-cp-sending-to-sbc-causes.

[6] Southern Baptist Convention, "History of the Division of Cooperative Program Funds Between All State Conventions and the SBC," Cooperative Program page, accessed June 7, 2017, http://www.sbc.net/pdf/cp/CPStatistics/HistoryOfDivisionCPFundsBetweenAllStates.pdf.

the Red Cross. Through the Cooperative Program, local Southern Baptist churches participate in these wide-ranging ministries.

Recent Changes in SBC Structure

The Southern Baptist Convention was established in 1845 and the Cooperative Program in 1925. It would be an understatement to say much has changed since then. Through the years, Southern Baptists have reacted to these changes and made adjustments to the structure of the convention and the flow of Cooperative Program funds. It is beyond the scope of this book to explore all of these changes. However, as we consider the SBC, it is important to reflect on two of the most recent changes in SBC structure.

Covenant for a New Century and the Great Commission Resurgence

At the end of the twentieth century, Southern Baptists emerged from a two-decade denominational battle known as the Conservative Resurgence. This conflict was public and at times bitter. It ended with new convention leadership in place and led to the establishment of several new Baptist bodies, including the Cooperative Baptist Fellowship. As the heat from this battle settled down and Southern Baptists approached their sesquicentennial anniversary, we became aware of the need to re-structure and renew the convention. The result, the Covenant for a New Century, became what Brand and Hankins called "the largest reorganization in SBC history."[7]

During the 1993 meeting of the SBC in Houston, Texas, Southern Baptists established the Program and Structure Committee and tasked it with the responsibility of studying convention structures and making recommendations for change. The committee presented its findings at the 1995 SBC meeting in Atlanta, Georgia. Its report highlighted that the mission of the convention "has stood unaltered for 150 years—a century and a half of faithful service and God blessed cooperation. . . . Even in this age of transformation, the mission of our convention remains the same—to cooperate in mission and ministry so that the gospel of Jesus Christ may be preached throughout the world." In other words, the Southern Baptist Convention, even after 150 years, has remained true to its original purpose. Yet to continue achieving that purpose, the committee recommended several changes.

First, the committee proposed that Southern Baptists adopt a new mission statement:

---

[7] Chad Owen Brand and David E. Hankins, *One Sacred Effort: The Cooperative Program of the Southern Baptist Convention* (Nashville: B&H, 2005), 125.

> The Southern Baptist Convention exists to facilitate, extend, and enlarge the Great Commission ministries of Southern Baptist Churches, to the glory of God the Father, under the Lordship of Jesus Christ, upon the authority of the Holy Scriptures, and empowered by the Holy Spirit.[8]

Along with this affirmation of the SBC's mission, the committee recommended a streamlined structure, reducing the number of convention entities from 19 to 12. This restructuring was accomplished by eliminating several entities and reassigning their responsibilities to those that remained.[9] In the end, the Southern Baptist Convention dissolved the Brotherhood Commission, Education Commission, Historical Commission, Home Mission Board, and Radio and Television Commission. The work of home missions, the Brotherhood Commission, and the Radio and Television Commission were all reassigned to the newly formed North American Mission Board. The work of the Historical Commission's Southern Baptist Historical Library and Archives became the responsibility of the Council of Seminary Presidents. The committee also recommended name changes for two entities: the Christian Life Commission became the Ethics and Religious Liberty Commission, and the Foreign Mission Board became the International Mission Board. Finally, the responsibility for promoting convention cooperation and the Cooperative Program became the responsibility of the Executive Committee.

At the end of the twentieth century, Southern Baptists restructured themselves for greater efficiency. Despite these changes, the SBC maintained a commitment to its original values and vision. These changes were implemented in 1997.

The Great Commission Resurgence and the Great Commission Task Force

On April 16, 2009, Daniel Akin preached a sermon in chapel at Southeastern Baptist Theological Seminary, laying out what he called "Axioms of a Great Commission Resurgence." This message was a call for Southern Baptists to refocus and restructure to more effectively fulfill the Great Commission. He observed, "Many of the issues we [Southern Baptists] are emphasizing and debating are interesting things, but they are not the most important things. They don't line up well with the priorities we find revealed in Holy Scripture. The result: we are fractured and factionalizing. We are confused, having lost our spiritual compass."[10] The message reflected the sentiments of a movement that led to change within the SBC.

---

[8] The Executive Committee of the Southern Baptist Convention, "Final Report: Implementation Task Force," http://www.sbcec.org/history/pdf/covenant%20for%20new%20centuryv4.pdf, June 16, 1997.
[9] Ibid.
[10] Daniel Akin, "Axioms for a Great Commission Resurgence," DanielAkin.com, accessed June 7, 2017, http://www.danielakin.com/wp-content/uploads/2009/04/acts-1-4-8-axioms-for-a-great-commission-resurgence-tt2.pdf.

At the 2009 meeting of the SBC in Louisville, Kentucky, messengers authorized President Johnny Hunt to establish a Great Commission Task Force charged with bringing a report to the 2010 convention concerning "how Southern Baptists can work more faithfully and effectively together in serving Christ through the Great Commission."[11] The task force was led by Ronnie Floyd, a pastor from Arkansas, and met frequently throughout 2009–2010. To encourage honest dialogue, the task force agreed to have the minutes of their meetings sealed for 15 years. The task force made a presentation that included seven recommendations adopted by the convention in 2010.

First, the task force suggested a change to the convention's mission statement. The new mission statement read, "As a convention of churches, our missional vision is to present the Gospel of Jesus Christ to every person in the world and to make disciples of all the nations."

The task force also recommended a set of core values:

CHRIST-LIKENESS
We depend on the transforming power of the Holy Spirit, the Word of God, and prayer to make us more like Jesus Christ.

TRUTH
We stand together in the truth of God's inerrant Word, celebrating the faith once for all delivered to the saints.

UNITY
We work together in love for the sake of the Gospel.

RELATIONSHIPS
We consider others more important than ourselves.

TRUST
We tell one another the truth in love and do what we say we will do.

FUTURE
We value Southern Baptists of all generations and embrace our responsibility to pass this charge to a rising generation in every age, faithful until Jesus comes.

---

[11] ABPNews, "SBC Re-Elects Johnny Hunt as President," Baptist News Global, June 24, 2009, https://baptist news.com/article/sbc-re-elects-johnny-hunt-as-president-3/#.WWiyyojyuUk.

LOCAL CHURCH
We believe the local church is given the authority, power, and responsibility to present the Gospel of Jesus Christ to every person in the world.

KINGDOM
We join other Christ-followers for the Gospel, the Kingdom of Christ, and the glory of God.

Each of these was intended to guide how Southern Baptists relate to one another and approach our mission.

Second, the task force recommended that Southern Baptists recognize a new stewardship category called Great Commission Giving to reinforce the importance of cooperative giving through all channels of Southern Baptist cooperation. The task force recommended that all funds given by churches through the Cooperative Program or designated to SBC, state convention, or local association causes be considered Great Commission Giving and indicated as such on reports.

Third, the task force made recommendations intended to increase the effectiveness of convention missionary efforts. First, the North American Mission Board was asked to make church planting its main priority. This was accompanied by a recommendation that existing cooperative agreements between the NAMB and state conventions be phased out and replaced with new partnership agreements. The task force also recommended that the International Mission Board begin working inside North America on behalf of unreached and underserved people groups who have immigrated to America. This would require greater partnership between the NAMB and the IMB than had previously been practiced.

Fourth, the task force recommended that the responsibility of promoting the Cooperative Program be transferred from the Executive Committee to the state conventions. This was a reversal of the Covenant for a New Century. According to the task force report, the reason for this proposed change was "straightforward and easy to see. The state conventions have the mechanisms in place to collect funds and promote the Cooperative Program."[12] Along with this, the task force also challenged state conventions to create a plan to "return to the historic ideal of 50/50 Cooperative Program distribution between the state convention [and SBC]."[13]

Finally, the task force recommended that the traditional allocation designated to the International Mission Board be raised from 50 percent to 51 percent. This recommended increase was intended to remind Southern Baptists that international

---

[12] *Annual of the 2010 Southern Baptist Convention* (Executive Committee of the Southern Baptist Convention, 2010), http://www.sbcec.org/bor/2010/2010sbcannual.pdf, 86.

[13] William Thornton, "Financial Statistics," SBC Voices, June 12, 2017, http://sbcvoices.com/the-two-most-important-numbers-in-sbc-financial-statistics/.

missions remains the priority of the convention. The report was ratified and the recommendations were then sent to different entities for consideration.[14]

Southern Baptists have not fully implemented all of these changes. Yet, because of the recommendations, the SBC Executive Committee proposed in 2011 the establishment of Great Commission Giving and revisions to the NAMB and IMB ministry assignments. Messengers adopted both recommendations, and the IMB began work among unreached people groups in North America. Further, the Executive Committee reduced its portion of CP funds so the convention could begin to forward 50.41 percent of CP receipts to the IMB. State conventions increased the average percentage of funds forwarded to SBC causes from 36.55 percent in 2008 to approximately 38 percent by 2014.[15]

The adjustments within the SBC that came about because of the Great Commission Task Force are the most recent attempts by Southern Baptists to maximize their cooperative missions. These changes highlight that cooperation is more than financial partnership. It also includes joint participation in the actual work. The next section briefly examines the work of Southern Baptist entities and shows how they are supported by Cooperative Program giving as well as how they encourage cooperation between churches in the advancement of the mission of the convention.

SOUTHERN BAPTIST CONVENTION ENTITIES AND THEIR WORK

The first Southern Baptist Convention was composed of 327 delegates. According to Leon McBeth, these delegates "included only 293 persons since some represented more than one church or society. . . . Of the 293 present, 273 came from the three states of Georgia, South Carolina, and Virginia."[16] From this rather small beginning, the Southern Baptist Convention has become the largest Protestant denomination in the world. Today Southern Baptists boast of more than 50,000 churches and church-type missions throughout North America. The North American Mission Board (NAMB) houses employees in Alpharetta, Georgia, and supports missionary activities in every state in the United States as well as Canada and several protectorates. The International Mission Board (IMB), headquartered in Richmond, Virginia, sends thousands of missionaries (long-, mid-, and short-term) to nearly every country in the world. The IMB is the largest denominational mission-sending agency in the world.

Southern Baptists also support the Ethics and Religious Liberty Commission (ERLC) with offices in Nashville, Tennessee; Washington, DC; and the Middle East (Cyprus). This Commission is responsible for advocating religious liberty and

[14] A fuller description of the GCR Task Force recommendations can be read in 2010 *Annual*. Ibid., 78.
[15] David Roach, "GCR after 5 Years: 'Satisfied' but Still Challenges," Baptist Press, August 11, 2015, http://www.bpnews.net/45287/gcr-after-5-years-satisfied-but-still-challenges.
[16] McBeth, *The Baptist Heritage*, 388.

lobbying United States politicians regarding Southern Baptist ethical concerns. Lifeway Christian Resources (formerly the Baptist Sunday School Board) produces educational material for Southern Baptist churches and is also one of the world's largest publishers of Christian material. GuideStone Financial Resources (formerly the Annuity Board) assists churches, denominational entities, and other ministries with retirement plan services, insurance coverage, and investment programs. The Southern Baptist Convention also supports six seminaries throughout the United States, educating thousands of men and women for service around the world and in local churches. The Executive Committee acts for the SBC between annual meetings in all matters not otherwise provided for and facilitates support for worldwide missions and ministries.

McBeth was certainly correct when he noted, "The 'delegates' who met in Augusta, Georgia, in May 1845 to form the Southern Baptist Convention would hardly recognize their creation today. . . . The Convention of 1845 had only two general boards, no commissions, seminaries, institutions, or standing committees. They had no headquarters, no budget, and no continuing officers between sessions. . . . The name remains, but almost everything else has changed."[17]

The Cooperative Program provides a mechanism that allows Southern Baptists to be involved in international and North American missions and to both educate Southern Baptist ministers and help Southern Baptists respond in a Christian manner to a shifting culture. The paragraphs that follow will provide you with a general overview of the Southern Baptist Convention entities, those that receive Cooperative Program funding and those that do not. To assist you, each entry notes a website that supplies complete and up-to-date information.

SBC Entities Receiving Support from the Cooperative Program

International Mission Board (IMB) www.imb.org
(received 51.41 percent of 2015–2016 SBC CP allocations)[18]

The IMB, headquartered in Richmond, Virginia, is responsible for leading Southern Baptists in global missions. Per the IMB's website, its purpose is to "partner with churches to empower limitless missionary teams who are making disciples and multiplying churches among unreached peoples and places for the glory of God." Through the years, the specific strategies have changed as opportunities present themselves; however, the core commitment of the IMB is to lead Southern Baptists

---

[17] McBeth, "Cooperation and Crisis as Shapers of Southern Baptist Identity," 35 (see intro., n. 7).
[18] Receipt percentages taken from "Love in Action," Southern Baptist Convention website, accessed June 7, 2017, http://www.sbc.net/cp/loveinaction.asp.

to engage all of the people groups in the world. Currently, Southern Baptists support nearly 4,000 missionaries around the world. Because of a very real concern for missionary safety, it is impossible to specify where all these men and women are deployed; however, it is probably safe to assume that Southern Baptist missions reach into every country in the world.

Along with financial support received through the Cooperative Program, the IMB is also funded by a special offering named after one of the most famous Southern Baptist missionaries, Charlotte (Lottie) Moon. The Lottie Moon Christmas Offering for International Missions is an annual fund that traditionally has been collected by Southern Baptists during the Christmas season each year. This fund is promoted by the Woman's Missionary Union and supplies almost 60 percent of the total operating budget for the IMB.

It is important to remember that the IMB is not merely a missionary-sending agency or society. It is a means through which Southern Baptist churches cooperate to fulfill the Great Commission.

North American Mission Board (NAMB) www.namb.net
(received 22.79 percent of 2015–2016 SBC CP allocations)

The NAMB is responsible for leading Southern Baptists in church planting and evangelism in the United States, Canada, and their territories. The home office is in Alpharetta, Georgia. As with the IMB, the specific strategies of the NAMB change to maximize opportunities and better accomplish the mission of Southern Baptists in North America.

Recently, the NAMB structured its work in two main divisions. The Send Network is responsible for helping Southern Baptist churches with evangelism and church planting as well as training missionaries, church planters, and chaplains. The Send Network concentrates most of its efforts on 32 of the most strategic and unreached areas in North America. These are known as "Send Cities."

Send Relief extends Christian care and social ministry through local churches, meeting physical needs and creating a bridge for the gospel. The ministries of this division include disaster relief, care for widows and orphans, hunger relief, and much more. These ministries happen as the NAMB cooperates with local churches, associations, state conventions, and other networks. As with the IMB, the NAMB is not merely a missionary society or agency; it is Southern Baptists cooperating to see North America impacted by the good news of Jesus.

While the NAMB receives Cooperative Program support, 49 percent of its operating budget comes through the Annie Armstrong Easter Offering for North American Missions. This offering is named after the founder and first corresponding secretary of the Woman's Missionary Union (WMU). Though this offering can be collected throughout the year, it has traditionally been collected around Easter and promoted by the WMU.

Seminaries
(All seminaries combined received 21.92 percent of 2015–2016 SBC CP allocations)

Southern Baptists also support six seminaries through the Cooperative Program.

- **Southern Baptist Theological Seminary** (www.sbts.edu): founded 1859, located in Louisville, Kentucky
- **Southwestern Baptist Theological Seminary** (www.swbts.edu): founded 1908, located in Fort Worth, Texas
- **New Orleans Baptist Theological Seminary** (www.nobts.edu): founded 1917, located in New Orleans, Louisiana
- **Gateway Seminary of the Southern Baptist Convention** (www.gs.edu): founded 1944,[19] located in Ontario, California
- **Southeastern Baptist Theological Seminary** (www.sebts.edu): founded 1951, located in Wake Forest, North Carolina
- **Midwestern Baptist Theological Seminary** (www.mbts.edu): founded 1957, located in Kansas City, Missouri

These seminaries provide a broad range of educational opportunities, from undergraduate through doctoral degrees, for men and women who are pursuing God's call to some type of church- or mission field–based ministry. Through our seminaries, Southern Baptists provide educated and trained leaders for local churches. The Council of Seminary Presidents also governs the Southern Baptist Historical Library and Archives and the Seminary Extension program, both located in the SBC Building in Nashville.

More than 20 percent of the Cooperative Program funds are distributed among the six seminaries. The goal is to provide quality theological education at the lowest cost possible. The importance of cooperation in theological education is often overlooked. Southern Baptist cooperation allows seminarians to prepare for ministry with significantly lower tuition than their peers at schools that do not receive Cooperative Program support. This enables graduates from SBC seminaries to limit their student loan debt, making it easier for them to follow God's call to small churches, rural areas, expensive urban areas, and other church-planting settings. When Southern Baptists cooperate, we make it possible for churches in different settings to call well-trained men and women to serve them. Together we support God's mission through our seminaries.

---

[19] Previously Golden Gate Seminary. The name was officially changed at the SBC meeting in St. Louis, June 2015.

Ethics and Religious Liberty Commission (ERLC) www.erlc.com
(received 1.65 percent of 2015–2016 SBC CP allocations)

The ERLC was established in 1913 as the Social Service Commission. It became a convention entity and was renamed the Christian Life Commission in 1953. The name was changed to Ethics and Religious Liberty Commission in 1997 as part of the Covenant for a New Century. The ERLC articulates the views of the Southern Baptist Convention in the public policy arena and equips Southern Baptist churches to understand and speak with confidence and Christian kindness to the ethical and social issues of the day. It is important to recognize that the ERLC is not merely a public policy arm. Its mission is established by and rooted in God's mission of redemption through Jesus Christ for the nations. For this reason, the ERLC seeks to approach social issues in ways that demonstrate the relevance and goodness of the Christian message. The ERLC receives a portion of its budget through the Cooperative Program. The remainder of its budget is generated through donations and purchase of resources.

Executive Committee www.sbcec.org
(received 2.99 percent of 2015–2016 CP allocations)

The Executive Committee was founded in 1917 to perform administrative duties on behalf of the convention while it is not in session and to carry out a limited number of program responsibilities. Today, the committee is composed of 83 members elected by the convention from qualified states and regions. The Executive Committee employs a staff in its Nashville, Tennessee, office to help carry out its duties. Among the committee's responsibilities are receiving and distributing Cooperative Program funds for SBC causes; promoting the Cooperative Program; planning and managing the SBC annual meeting; publishing the convention annual; handling legal matters; operating Baptist Press, the convention's news service; and assisting convention committees.

SBC Entities Not Receiving Support from the Cooperative Program

GuideStone Financial Resources www.guidestone.org

GuideStone was established in 1918 as the Relief and Annuity Board of the Southern Baptist Convention. Its mission is to provide financial resources and help for Southern Baptist ministers and their spouses. These financial resources include retirement plans, life and health insurance, personal investment accounts, and even financial and retirement advisement. GuideStone works hard to make sure all investments are consistent with the Christian worldview and biblical principles. Their mission is to help Christian ministers achieve a degree of financial stability so these men and women can serve the church with minimal financial distraction.

In 2007 GuideStone chose to stop receiving Cooperative Program support. Before this, all Cooperative Program funds were used to support Mission Dignity, a ministry to ministers, denominational workers, and their widows who face financial crises in retirement. Currently, this ministry is supported through individual and corporate donations.

LifeWay Christian Resources www.lifeway.com

In 1891, Southern Baptists established the Baptist Sunday School Board with the responsibility of publishing and distributing Sunday school material to Southern Baptist churches. Over the years it began publishing more than Sunday school and church education material. In 1998, the convention changed the Baptist Sunday School Board's name to LifeWay Christian Resources to reflect the fact that it produces more than Sunday school literature. LifeWay continues to provide education material to churches, but its influence is much broader. Today, LifeWay is one of the largest providers of Christian resources and services in the world.

All financial support comes through the sale of resources and services. In fact, Lifeway reinvests all profit above operating expenses back into mission and ministry opportunities around the world. B&H Publishing Group serves as the Bible and book publishing arm of LifeWay and is one of the largest Christian publishing companies in the world. LifeWay also operates the Ridgecrest Conference Center in North Carolina, which provides a location for retreats and conferences. LifeWay Research monitors trends of interest to Southern Baptists and supplies pastors and churches with helpful information. LifeWay, though not supported by the Cooperative Program, serves as an important cooperative entity for Southern Baptists. Its goal is to provide resources to strengthen and support churches of different sizes, languages, and needs.

Woman's Missionary Union (WMU) www.wmu.com

The WMU was established in 1888 as an auxiliary of the SBC. Its purpose is to elicit prayer and financial support for missions, as well as provide missionary education for women, teenagers, and children. Today the WMU leads Southern Baptist churches to support missions by communicating prayer needs, supplying age-graded mission education programs, and promoting missionary opportunities. The most visible, and some might argue the most significant, contribution to Southern Baptist cooperative missions comes in the form of support-raising. Every year, WMU promotes the two largest mission offerings in the convention: the Lottie Moon Christmas

Offering for International Missions and the Annie Armstrong Easter Offering for North American Missions. Since 1956, the WMU has raised more than $2.5 billion for Southern Baptist missions.

COOPERATION: A WAY FORWARD FOR SOUTHERN BAPTISTS

When Akin preached "Axioms of a Great Commission Resurgence," he bemoaned that too many Southern Baptists were distracted by petty denominational squabbles. His challenge was for Southern Baptists to simplify and prioritize around what he labeled a "3-legged stool," consisting of "church planting in the United States, pioneer missions around the world and theological education that starts in the seminaries but finds its way into the local church."[20] Whether or not one agrees with all of Akin's assessments, Southern Baptists seem to agree with his emphasis on the three cooperative priorities for Southern Baptists. A 2008 survey conducted by Life-Way Research showed that Southern Baptist pastors considered these areas matters of high priority.[21] Some 93 percent of pastors surveyed said pioneer missions are an essential or high priority for SBC Cooperative Program support, and almost half stated that direct support of and involvement in international missions should remain a priority. More than 85 percent stated that the development and implementation of an evangelism strategy for penetrating lostness in North America is an essential or high priority for Southern Baptists, while more than 50 percent agreed that church planting in cities and towns in the United States is a priority. Finally, when asked about the importance of providing theological education for pastors, missionaries, church planters, and denominational workers, 53 percent agreed that this should be an essential or high priority. These statistics evidence the unity Southern Baptists possess surrounding our Cooperative Program.

There may be things on which we disagree, and there are matters that we will continue to debate, but the essential mission of the convention is a common ground. In the chapters that follow, we will discover that these priorities—church planting, reaching the nations, and making disciples—are not only Southern Baptist priorities; they are foundational components of the mission of God. In essence, when we cooperate together in these convention endeavors, we join God in his mission to save the world through his redeemed church.

---

[20] Akin, "Axioms for a Great Commission Resurgence," 17–18.
[21] Information comes from research data as well as from Carol Pipes, "Pastors Value SBC's Cooperative Program," LifeWay, December 11, 2012, http://www.lifeway.com/Article/research-pastors-value-sbc-cooperative-program.

PART II

GOD'S MISSION AND THE MISSION OF HIS PEOPLE

T his section explores important biblical and theological themes. The goal is to present a biblical foundation for Southern Baptist cooperative efforts. The previous section portrayed the SBC cooperation through historical lenses. This section views it through biblical lenses. It is important to recognize that, as far as I can determine, the arguments made in this section were not used by early Southern Baptists in the development and support of the Cooperative Program or SBC cooperative structure. I am seeking to show today's Southern Baptists, young and old, why our denominational cooperative efforts are not only practically beneficial, but also biblical. I hope this section will be an encouragement as Southern Baptists engage in God's mission in our changing times. Finally, this section will challenge those who are considering walking away from the convention to consider their decisions through the lenses of Scripture.

John Stott once famously said, "Our God is a missionary God." Though Stott was not a Baptist, the truth behind this statement is the driving force behind Southern Baptist efforts. The mission of our God is his loving pursuit of fallen humanity. It is accomplished through Christ and proclaimed by his church. Every local church exists *by* God's mission and *for* God's mission. The flow of this section can be summarized with a series of simple statements:

- Our one God has a mission in this world.
- The mission of God establishes a redeemed people, the church.
- The church is a universal body made up of local expressions, each of which is autonomous and responsible to fulfill his mission.
- Local churches are commissioned into God's mission as part of the global body of Christ. This missionary work is best accomplished in partnership with the global church. Cooperation between local churches is the natural and anticipated means for accomplishing this mission.

Of all the denominations in the world, Southern Baptists are structured to most fully engage in God's mission. I recognize this is a bold statement. But as you read these pages, I trust you will see why I make this claim.

SOUTHERN BAPTIST THEOLOGICAL PRIORITIES

Even though Southern Baptists do not have a reputation for being highly educated or deeply reflective, it would be a mistake to assume theology is unimportant to us. In fact, one result of the conservative resurgence was a recognition of the importance of conservative evangelical theology. This emphasis has created a generation of younger Southern Baptists for whom it is not sufficient to appeal to tradition or history for motivation. This new generation of Southern Baptists requires, and is looking for, a theological reason for maintaining our convention structure and cooperative identity.

The most recent update of the Baptist Faith and Message, adopted in June 2000, includes several significant changes. These changes reflect points of emphasis for Southern Baptists. A survey of what the Baptist Faith and Message says concerning the Scriptures, the local church, salvation, and our mission will provide insight into important Southern Baptist priorities.

The Scriptures

Of first order, Southern Baptists are *people of the Book*, affirming without hesitation or apology a belief that the Scriptures are trustworthy and authoritative. The Baptist Faith and Message (BF&M) says:

> The Holy Bible was written by men divinely inspired and is God's rev-elation of Himself to man. It is a perfect treasure of divine instruction. It has God for its author, salvation for its end, and truth, without any mixture of error, for its matter. Therefore, all Scripture is totally true and trustworthy. It reveals the principles by which God judges us, and therefore is, and will remain to the end of the world, the true center of Christian union, and the supreme standard by which all human con-duct, creeds, and religious opinions should be tried. All Scripture is a testimony to Christ, who is Himself the focus of divine revelation.[1]

In this statement, Southern Baptists included several adjustments to express what we believe about the Bible. First, in the previous (1963) version, this section reads, "The Holy Bible was written by men divinely inspired and is the record of God's revelation of Himself to man." In the most recent version, the phrase "is the record of" was eliminated. Albert Mohler, who served on the committee that drafted the BF&M 2000, wrote, "We removed the word 'record' in order to remove confusion about the nature of God's revelation in the Bible. The Bible is not merely a record of revelation. It is revelation itself."[2] This decision clarifies what Southern Baptists mean when we say that the Scriptures are the Word of God.

Second, each of the previous versions of the BF&M declares the Bible has "truth, without any mixture of error, for its matter." The BF&M 2000 kept this phrase but

---

[1] Southern Baptist Convention, The Baptist Faith and Message (2000), "I. The Scriptures," http://www.sbc.net/bfm2000/bfm2000.asp.

[2] R. Albert Mohler, "The Scriptures, BF&M Article 1" in *An Exposition from the Faculty of the Southern Baptist Theological Seminary on the Baptist Faith and Message 2000*, ed. Lawrence Smith (Louisville: Southern Baptist Theological Seminary, 2001), 1.

added: "Therefore, all Scripture is totally true and trustworthy." This addition makes plain what Southern Baptists mean when we use the word *inerrancy* to describe the Bible. According to Joseph Wooddell, "[Inerrancy] simply means that [the Bible] makes no false . . . claims; if the Bible makes an affirmation, then that affirmation is true."[3] Inerrancy rests on the fact that the Bible is divine revelation; it is not simply the work of inspired men. Mohler wrote, "Southern Baptists will not retreat from the high ground of biblical authority and theological integrity. . . . Southern Baptists are determined to face the future from the high ground of biblical faithfulness."[4] The doctrine of Scripture is of primary importance to Southern Baptists. It is the final authority on belief and action.

The Church

Baptist theologian John Hammett has observed that "most other Baptist distinctives grow out of their doctrine of the church."[5] Our belief that church membership is only available to baptized believers determines how we govern the church, disciple members, and also how we engage the world around us. According to the Baptist Faith and Message:

> A New Testament church of the Lord Jesus Christ is an autonomous local congregation of baptized believers, associated by covenant in the faith and fellowship of the gospel; observing the two ordinances of Christ, governed by His laws, exercising the gifts, rights, and privileges invested in them by His Word, and seeking to extend the gospel to the ends of the earth. Each congregation operates under the Lordship of Christ through democratic processes. In such a congregation, each member is responsible and accountable to Christ as Lord. Its scriptural officers are pastors and deacons. While both men and women are gifted for service in the church, the office of pastor is limited to men as qualified by Scripture.

> The New Testament speaks also of the church as the Body of Christ which includes all of the redeemed of all the ages, believers from every tribe, and tongue, and people, and nation.[6]

---

[3] Joseph D. Wooddell, "Article I: The Scriptures" in *Baptist Faith and Message 2000: Critical Issues in America's Largest Protestant Denomination*, ed. Douglas K. Blount and Joseph D. Wooddell (Lanham, MD: Rowman & Littlefield, 2007), 3.

[4] Mohler, "The Scriptures," 1.

[5] John S. Hammett, *Biblical Foundations for Baptist Churches* (Grand Rapids: Kregel, 2005), 21.

[6] Southern Baptist Convention, The Baptist Faith and Message (2000), "VI. The Church."

This statement has several important revisions from the previous statement. As we consider the mission of God, three important questions need to be considered: What is the church? Who is the church? What is the church supposed to do?

In answer to the question, What is the church? Southern Baptists affirm the doctrine of local church autonomy. By this, we mean that each local church is the body of Christ in a specific place, and as such is not accountable to any other earthly authority. Local churches have authority and responsibility over church discipline, doctrine, and government. Belief in the autonomy of the local church does not stem from a spirit of rebellion or independence. It is rooted in the answer to the next question, Who is the church?

One hallmark of Baptist belief is the unwavering conviction that the local church consists only of confessing, baptized Christians. Church membership is reserved for those old enough to profess saving faith in Christ, followed by baptism by immersion. According to Hammett, belief in regenerate church membership "was the root [of] Baptist origins."[7] Southern Baptists stand where Baptists have always stood. The church, then, is God's redeemed people. It exists as the result, or object, of God's redemptive mission.

The answers to the questions, What is the church? and, Who is the church? shape the answer to the third question, What is the church supposed to do? All local churches are equipped to, and completely responsible for governing themselves, supporting themselves, and practicing the ordinances. Churches are equally responsible for fulfilling the missionary mandates of Scripture. Greg Wills has noted, "All the members jointly have responsibility to do everything that Christ commanded the churches to do."[8] When the BF&M speaks of cooperation between churches, these cooperative efforts are always, and only, extensions of local church ministry. The BF&M 2000 states, "Christ's people should . . . organize such associations and conventions as may best secure cooperation for the great objects of the Kingdom of God. Such organizations have no authority over one another or over the churches." Boards and agencies are all servants of the church, not the other way around."[9] In a later chapter, we will explore the relationship between the universal and the local church. For now, it is important to recognize that, though Southern Baptists affirm the existence and importance of the universal body of Christ, our structure and theological statements are careful to avoid undermining the autonomy and responsibility of the local church.

---

[7] Ibid., 98.
[8] Greg Wills, "The Church, BF&M Article 6" in Smith, *An Exposition from the Faculty of The Southern Baptist Theological Seminary on The Baptist Faith and Message 2000*, 22.
[9] Baptist Faith and Message 2000, art. 14.

Salvation

Third, Southern Baptists assert that salvation is only possible by faith alone in Christ alone.

> Salvation involves the redemption of the whole man, and is offered freely to all who accept Jesus Christ as Lord and Saviour, who by His own blood obtained eternal redemption for the believer. In its broadest sense salvation includes regeneration, justification, sanctification, and glorification. There is no salvation apart from personal faith in Jesus Christ as Lord.[10]

The BF&M 2000 adds the phrase "There is no salvation apart from personal faith in Jesus." According to Mohler, this addition is not something the framers of the 1925 or 1963 versions of the BF&M would have rejected; however, at the end of the twentieth century, several movements made it necessary to provide a clear statement concerning the exclusivity of Christ and the requirement of personal response. "This sentence," he wrote, "clearly precludes any form of inclusivism or universalism—any suggestion that a sinner can be saved apart from a conscious response of faith in the Lord Jesus Christ prior to the sinner's death."[11] Southern Baptists have established a boundary for belief: sinners are only declared right with God through personal, conscious belief in the finished work of Christ. This statement about salvation sets the framework for Southern Baptist belief about the mission of God and the church.

Missions and Evangelism

According to the BF&M 2000:

> It is the duty and privilege of every follower of Christ and of every church of the Lord Jesus Christ to endeavor to make disciples of all nations. The new birth of man's spirit by God's Holy Spirit means the birth of love for others. Missionary effort on the part of all rests thus upon a spiritual necessity of the regenerate life, and is expressly and repeatedly commanded in the teachings of Christ. The Lord Jesus Christ has commanded the preaching of the gospel to all nations. It is the duty of every child of God to seek constantly to win the lost to Christ by

---

[10] See Douglas K. Blount and Joseph D. Wooddell, eds., *Baptist Faith and Message 2000: Critical Issues in America's Largest Protestant Denomination* (Lanham, MD: Rowman & Littlefield, 2007), 207.

[11] R. Albert Mohler, "Article IV: The Doctrine of Salvation" in Blount and Wooddell, *Baptist Faith and Message 2000*, 40.

verbal witness undergirded by a Christian lifestyle, and by other methods in harmony with the gospel of Christ.[12]

In this revision, Southern Baptists made one important change. They replaced
the phrase "by personal effort" with the phrase "by *verbal witness undergirded by
a Christian lifestyle.*"[13] According to Thom Rainer, this addition was "absolutely
needed, and . . . added a component to the mandate of missions and evangelism
that was conspicuously absent in previous statements."[14] This phrase was added to
counter a prevailing notion of so-called *lifestyle evangelism*, which downplays the
importance of a verbal witness.

Along with emphasis on the necessity of verbal witness, the BF&M 2000 also
addressed the scope of the church's mission by adding the phrase "The Lord Jesus
Christ has commanded the preaching of the gospel to all nations." According to
Keith Eitel, this phrase indicates Southern Baptists recognize that God's mission
does not focus on nation-states, but on the different people groups within national
borders. He noted, "The framers of the *Baptist Faith and Message 2000* indicate full
recognition of this scriptural emphasis that Southern Baptists must affirm in order
to demonstrate our obedience to the full implications of Christ's commissioning."[15]
With these two changes, Southern Baptists are doing more than emphasizing a denominational value. They are making a theological statement about the eternal state
of unevangelized people. Without personal, conscious faith in Christ, all people,
including those born in countries with insufficient Christian presence, remain spir-
itually lost. It is the responsibility of all churches to seek to win everyone to Christ.

As noted earlier, our God is a missionary God. His church is a missionary people given the responsibility of proclaiming his message of salvation to the nations
so those who are lost can be saved and become members of this missionary body.
The chapters that follow present a biblical description of the mission of God. This
biblical vision forms the backbone of Southern Baptist cooperation: one God, one
mission, one universal church with many local expressions.

---

[12] Ibid., 218.
[13] Article XI, Baptist Faith and Message 2000, "Comparison of 1925, 1963 and 2000 Baptist Faith and Message"; emphasis added.
[14] Thom Rainer, "Evangelism and Missions, BF&M Article 11" in Smith, *An Exposition from the Faculty of the
Southern Baptist Theological Seminary on The Baptist Faith and Message 2000*, 33.
[15] Keith Eitel, "Article IX: Evangelism and Missions" in Blount and Wooddell, *Baptist Faith and Message 2000*,
113.

4

Our God Is a Missionary God

According to Eph 1:9, one blessing of salvation is that God "[makes] known to us the mystery of his will." Before redemption, we believed the central purpose of our lives was to please and protect ourselves. However, according to these verses, believers have been adopted into God's family (Eph 1:5) and brought into the counsel of our Creator. Our purpose has been transformed and our life agenda has been altered. The apostle Paul tells us that Christians are invited into God's global mission of bringing everything back into conformity with his will. According to Eph 1:10, God has a timetable. In the fullness of time, he will bring everything in heaven and earth together in Christ. However, in this age, during the time before God establishes his ultimate rule, our purpose is to participate in this mission. This chapter will provide an overview of God's mission and explain God's purpose to redeem people from all nations.

God reveals himself, his will, and his purposes through his Word. So, as we seek to understand our God and his mission, we must look in the pages of Scripture. The Bible is 66 books written over thousands of years by dozens of different authors. It traces the histories of nations and peoples, and it contains some of the richest religious teachings ever penned. It describes God's relentless pursuit to rescue fallen people from the penalty and power of sin. God's mission is to create for himself a special people who are his representatives in this world. God's people serve as the agents of his mission until all of history culminates in his final kingdom.

God's Mission Revealed

God's mission can be seen in the opening pages of the Bible. Here we read of God's creation of this world and everything in it. The pinnacle of creation was humanity, man and woman. After creating them and bringing them together, God declared this world to be "very good" (Gen 1:31). Despite God's bold declaration, we no longer live in a "very good" world. Though some seasons of life are good, a brief look at our lives, the lives of those near us, the news, or our social media feeds is clear evidence that this world is broken. The world is no longer "very good." What happened?

The story of creation is followed closely by the story of what theologians call *the fall*. This single event destroyed the "very good" character of our world. In Genesis 2, Moses describes a perfect garden. The garden is filled with lush plants, plenty of water, gold, and precious gems. Everything is in perfect harmony; God walks and talks with his creation. Gen 2:17 says God pointed out one tree and told the man not to eat from that tree. However, as we all know, he *did* eat from that forbidden tree, and as a result, all of creation fell into chaos. The apostle Paul, reflecting on this event, would later write, "Just as sin entered the world through one man, and death through sin, in this way death spread to all people, because all sinned" (Rom 5:12). This one, seemingly simple act of rebellion against the will of God produced a world that, though it retains elements of its original goodness, is no longer "very good."

Immediately following this initial act of rebellion, both man and woman were overcome with shame, guilt, and fear. They hid their bodies from one another and also tried to hide from God. Their disobedience placed them under God's judgment. Let's look again at Romans 5 to see how Paul describes the consequences of this initial sin:

> 5:17: by the one man's trespass, death reigned . . .
> 5:18: through one trespass there is condemnation for everyone . . .
> 5:19: through one man's disobedience the many were made sinners . . .

The fall introduced physical, relational, and spiritual consequences to the world. Humanity chose to walk away from God, but he chose to pursue us.

A key verse in the opening pages of the Bible is Gen 3:15. God is speaking to the serpent, the source of temptation and the essence of evil. God promises, "I will put hostility between you and the woman, and between your offspring and her offspring. He will strike your head, and you will strike his heel." In this verse we see God's promise to rescue men and women. Here we have the unveiling of God's mission to destroy evil and sin through the work of a Son. This Son will be wounded (the serpent "will strike his heel"), but this wound will result in the crushing of the serpent's head. Paul explains, again in Romans 5:

> 5:17: how much more will those who receive the overflow of grace and the gift of righteousness reign in life through the one man, Jesus Christ.

5:18: through one righteous act there is justification leading to life for everyone.

5:19: through one man's obedience the many will be made righteous.

The mystery is revealed. God's mission is seen in Jesus Christ's ministry to rescue creation from the consequences of the fall. The next section will show how God's mission is carried out through a special people.

GOD'S MISSION THROUGH HIS PEOPLE

The story of God's mission continues through the narrative of Scripture. According to Christopher Wright, the entire Bible can be summed up in the central question, "What can God do about the sin and rebellion of the human race?"[1] Throughout the Old Testament, the careful reader finds hints of a future hope. There is the promise of one who is yet to come, someone who will set the world back in order. In Deut 18:15, Moses promised that God would send another prophet to whom the people must listen. In 2 Samuel 7, God promised David that through one of his sons, God would establish an eternal kingdom. The prophet Isaiah predicted that a servant of God would come. This servant would be stricken, punished, and bruised in order to absorb the punishment and penalty of human sinfulness (Isaiah 53). These three examples barely scratch the surface of Old Testament anticipation of God's coming Savior.

There is a second compelling storyline in the Old Testament as well, the story of God's mission of redemption through a chosen people. God's mission through his people begins in earnest in Genesis 12 when God sends Abram—later Abraham—from his home with the promise to make Abram's descendants into a great nation, which would, in turn, bless "all the peoples on earth" (Gen 12:3). The remainder of the Old Testament is the story of this chosen people, Israel, and its mission. Michael Goheen has noted that throughout the Old Testament, the Israelites struggled to keep their purpose in mind. They forgot "the missional purpose of election" and instead chose to emphasize "only privilege, salvation, and the status of being a recipient."[2] Israel misunderstood the purpose of its calling and failed in its responsibility to advance God's mission to bless the peoples of the earth.

God's selection of Israel was never simply about saving one nation among many. Rather, Israel was to serve as the agent of and platform for God's mission of bringing creation back into communion with him. The mission of God through Israel was what some missiologists have called *centripetal*; that is, attractional in nature. "The

---

[1] Christopher J. H. Wright, *The Mission of God: Unlocking the Bible's Grand Narrative* (Downers Grove, IL: InterVarsity Press, 2006), 195.

[2] Michael Goheen, *A Light to the Nations: The Missional Church and the Biblical Story* (Grand Rapids: Baker Academic, 2011), 31.

Mosaic social life of justice and mercy," Goheen observed, "is designed to arouse the admiration and envy of the nations."[3] Israel was to be a light to the nations; as it obeyed the covenant and experienced the presence of God, the nations would be drawn to its God. Despite this noble trajectory, the Old Testament tells the story of Israel's failure in this mission; the nation misunderstood the purpose of election and forsook its covenant with God. Rather than being a light and blessing to the nations, the Old Testament ends with God's chosen people in humiliation and exile. Yet even through this painful account of Israel's failure, readers can detect God's mission to save the nations through a chosen people.

GOD'S MISSION CONTINUES THROUGH CHRIST AND HIS CHURCH

The first line of the first book of the New Testament reads, "An account of the genealogy of Jesus Christ, the Son of David, the Son of Abraham" (Matt 1:1). With this simple phrase, the reader has the first signal that the Savior, the promised Son from Gen 3:15, has come into the world. He is Jesus of Nazareth.

The writers of all four gospels take great pains to show Jesus is the fulfillment of the Old Testament hope. Perhaps one of the most astounding claims came from the lips of John the Baptist. When he saw Jesus coming toward him, he told the crowd, "Here is the Lamb of God, who takes away the sin of the world!" (John 1:29). This bold claim declared that Jesus came to fulfill God's mission to rescue humanity from the curse of sin. Jesus was crucified to satisfy the wrath of God and fulfill the promise of Gen 3:15 that the Son would be wounded as he crushed the head of the tempter. This is certainly what Paul had in mind in Col 2:14–15 when he wrote, "He erased the certificate of debt, with its obligations, that was against us and opposed to us, and has taken it away by nailing it to the cross. He disarmed the rulers and authorities and disgraced them publicly; he triumphed over them through it."[4] It is important to recognize that, just as with God's salvation of Israel in the Old Testament, Jesus's work of redemption is not merely focused on individuals. Through his work of redemption, he is creating a people who are commissioned to reach the nations.

Missiologist David Bosch declared, "Salvation in Christ is salvation in the context of human society en route to a whole healed world."[5] God's work of redemption, saving fallen creation from the penalty and power of sin, has missional implications. Scot McKnight has noted that God's saving work "is not just something done to and for us, *it is something we participate in—in this work in the here and now*."[6] Those who

---

[3] Ibid., 42.

[4] This quote follows the alternate reading in the footnote of the CSB.

[5] David Bosch, *Transforming Mission: Paradigm Shifts in Theology of Mission* (Maryknoll, NY: Orbis Books, 1991), 399.

[6] Scot McKnight, *A Community Called Atonement* (Nashville: Abingdon Press, 2007), 30; emphasis in the original.

believe in Jesus become a special, redeemed people, who then participate in God's mission to all the peoples of the earth. Goheen has observed that the church, God's redeemed people, is called to fulfill the same mission God gave Israel. "The Old Testament story," he wrote, "points forward to a time when just such a people will be gathered and renewed—and through them, God's purposes will be fulfilled."[7] The church, then, is the extension and heir of the work God started in Israel. God's mission to bless the nations continues through Jesus, who promised that his disciples would be witnesses to the ends of the earth (Acts 1:8). The church is not a replacement of Israel but inherits Israel's missionary calling. Just as Israel was supposed to be a light to the nations, the church has been called and sent with the same mandate. The key difference is that Israel's mission was exclusively centripetal (attractional), whereas the church's mission is presented as both centripetal and centrifugal (come/ see and go/tell).

More will be said about the mission of the church in the next chapter. However, at this point, it is important to keep in mind that the Bible unveils the mission of God to rescue his lost creation from the brutal consequences of sin. Our God is a God with a mission. According to the verse with which we opened this chapter, Eph 1:10, his mission will ultimately be accomplished at some point in the future when he brings "everything together in Christ." Until that day, God's people, the church, are commissioned to proclaim the message of God's salvation to all nations.

SOUTHERN BAPTIST COOPERATION AND GOD'S MISSION

The Southern Baptist Convention was established in 1845 as a means for Baptists to participate in God's mission. In fact, one of our most cherished statements is found in the preamble of our constitution, where the purpose of the convention is summarized as "eliciting, combining, and directing the energies of the whole denomination in *one sacred effort*, for the propagation of the Gospel."[8] This statement is a reminder that missions is not a task invented by us. The mission belongs to our God. This is why it is *sacred*. We cooperate together in this mission because we are commissioned into God's mission. There is only one mission, and as God's people, cooperation must be our missional instinct.

There is no doubt that when Southern Baptists cooperate in missions, we accomplish much more than we can alone. However, our chief reason for cooperation should be centered in our participation in God's mission. In the next chapters, we will see that the biblical vision of the church on mission anticipates cooperation as a natural response to God's missionary mandate.

---

[7] Goheen, *A Light to the Nations*, 73.
[8] Original Constitution of the Southern Baptist Convention, emphasis added (see chap. 1, n. 19).

5

God's Mission and God's People

The previous chapter showed God has a mission; he is seeking to redeem the lost. The storyline of Scripture is composed of different events and covers thousands of years, but the Bible has one overarching theme: God's mission to redeem the nations and establish a people who work to fulfill his mission.

This chapter will look at New Testament teaching about the mission of the church. Previously, we saw that Baptist identity is rooted in answers to the questions, What is the church? and, Who can be a member? Southern Baptists have taken this question further, asking, What is the church to do in this lost and unevangelized world? The preamble of the SBC constitution states that our purpose is "eliciting, combining, and directing the energies of the whole denomination *in one sacred effort, for the propagation of the Gospel.*"[1]

Southern Baptists have established boards, entities, and programs to assist churches as they strive to accomplish this "sacred effort." The question we want to address in this chapter is, How does biblical teaching about the nature and ministry of the church encourage cooperation in the Southern Baptist Convention? The Bible presents a vision of local church unity as well as connection between churches. In this chapter, we will show that local church cooperation is an important means of fulfilling God's mission.

The Role of the Church in God's Mission

The Bible shows that the purpose of God's mission is to create a people who will worship him and make him known. This is evident at least as far back as God's call of Abram (Abraham). According to Gen 12:2, God promised to create from Abram

---

[1] Original Constitution of the Southern Baptist Convention, emphasis added. See http://www.sbc.net/aboutus/legal/constitution.asp to read the entire constitution of the SBC.

a "great nation." In other words, God's purpose in calling Abraham was not to high-light one person, or even one family. Instead, the focus of God's mission was to create a nation. Some may read this as a reference to the Hebrew people, but in the book of Galatians, the apostle Paul wrote, "Those who have faith, these are Abraham's sons" (3:7). The great nation God created consists of those who have placed their faith in Jesus. In the New Testament, such people are called "the church." In other words, the goal of God's mission is to build the church. The mission is successful as the church is established and expands to all nations.

Theologians use the terms *universal* and *local* to differentiate between two dis-tinct ways New Testament writers use the word *ekklésia*, which is translated "church." Most often, the word *church* is used of a group of believers gathered in a specific lo-cation.[2] For example, "the church of God at Corinth" (1 Cor 1:2), "the churches of Galatia" (Gal 1:2), or even "the church that meets in their home" (Rom 16:5). These refer to specific gatherings, or local churches.

There are other instances when the New Testament uses *church* to refer to a more abstract entity. Examples include Paul's comparison of marriage to Christ and the church in Eph 5:23 and his assertion in Col 1:18 that Christ is "the head of the body, the church." Another example can be found in Matt 16:18 when Jesus says, "I will build my church." These passages, and others like them, do not speak of a single, gathered body. Rather, they refer to the church in a universal sense.

The labels *local* and *universal* do not refer to distinct groups of people. *Local church* designates the physical assembling of the church in a particular place. *Universal church* references every person, throughout all times and all places, who has trusted Christ as Savior. The local church can be observed as an assembly on earth, while the universal church can only be observed in eternity. As Stanley Grenz ex-plains, the local church is "the local reality of the one church."[3] The local church is part of the universal church gathered locally in a specified location.

It is precisely at this point of relationship between the local and the univer-sal church that Southern Baptists find a theological basis for cooperation. How-ever, not all Southern Baptists have affirmed the concept of the universal church. Nineteenth-century Landmark Baptists rejected this idea and argued *church* should only be used in reference to a local body of believers that maintained the biblically prescribed order and structure. They were willing to accept as *church* only a local assembly that practiced regenerate membership and believer's baptism. Mark De-ver wrote, "One can get something of the seriousness of the [Landmark] contro-versy when it is noted that Basil Manly Jr.'s 1859 Abstract of Principles written for Southern Baptist Theological Seminary, lacked any affirmation of the existence of

---

[2] Hammett, *Biblical Foundations for Baptist Churches*, 70 (see the introduction to part 2, n. 4). Hammett, noted that *ekklésia* (and derivative terms) is used 114 times in the New Testament. The vast majority (at least 90 references) refer to a local assembly.

[3] Stanley Grenz, *Theology for the Community of God* (Grand Rapids: Eerdmans, 2000), 68.

the universal church–a matter which would have been uncontroversial among Baptists two or three decades earlier."[4] Although the Abstract of Principles is still used as a statement of faith for two Southern Baptist seminaries, the Baptist Faith and Message is utilized by all six and confirms Baptist belief in both the church universal and the local church:

> A New Testament church of the Lord Jesus Christ is an autonomous local congregation of baptized believers, associated by covenant in the faith and fellowship of the gospel; observing the two ordinances of Christ, governed by His laws, exercising the gifts, rights, and privileges invested in them by His Word, and seeking to extend the gospel to the ends of the earth. Each congregation operates under the Lordship of Christ through democratic processes. In such a congregation each member is responsible and accountable to Christ as Lord. Its scriptural officers are pastors and deacons. While both men and women are gifted for service in the church, the office of pastor is limited to men as qualified by Scripture.

> The New Testament speaks also of the church as the Body of Christ which includes all of the redeemed of all the ages, believers from every tribe, and tongue, and people, and nation.[5]

Southern Baptists emphasize the autonomy and authority of the local church. However, the BF&M makes clear that we also recognize the reality and importance of the universal church.

THE NATURE OF THE CHURCH: THE BODY OF CHRIST

Among the most helpful devices in the New Testament for teaching about the mission of the church are illustrative metaphors. For example, the church is described as a bride in Ephesians 5 and Revelation 19–20. The church is described as a building or temple in Ephesians 2 and 1 Peter 2. It is also described as a family or a new generation in Galatians 6, Ephesians 2, and 1 Peter 2.

Perhaps the most popular metaphor used in Scripture is the church as a body. Paul used this metaphor in Romans 12, 1 Corinthians 12, Ephesians 4, and Colossians 1, applying it to the universal as well as the local church. In each passage, this

---

[4] Mark Dever, "The Doctrine of the Church" in *Theology for the Church*, ed. Daniel Akin, Bruce Ashford, and Kenneth Keathley (Nashville: B&H Academic, 2014), nn. 110, 641.

[5] See "VI. The Church" under "Current Baptist Faith and Message Statement" in "Comparison of 1925, 1963 and 2000 Baptist Faith and Message," Southern Baptist Convention website, copyright 2017, http://www.sbc.net/bfm2000/bfmcomparison.asp.

metaphor highlights two key ideas. First, it is used to describe relationships between individual members within the church. Second, Paul used this metaphor to illustrate the relationship between Christ and the church as a whole; he is head of the body. The unity of the church and the headship of Christ are crucial for the health of the church and for its overall success in mission. This metaphor illustrates the basis for partnership in mission and church cooperation

The Ministry and Mission of the Church

Ephesians 4 and 1 Corinthians 12 use the body metaphor to show that unity and partnership rest on the common worship of God and his redemptive work. In these passages, Paul was concerned that the different ministries and gifts among members were creating division in the churches at Ephesus and Corinth. Relationship crises frequently bring ministry to a halt, and this is why Paul was addressing these churches. Even though the situation in each church was different, Paul's message to both congregations was the same: "Live out what you are in the gospel; be unified, because the church is one body." Paul made at least three foundational points that shape church unity and partnership in ministry.

1. The One Church Worships One God

First, Paul appealed for church unity based on the nature of God himself. John Stott wrote, "We should all be eager for some visible expression of Christian unity . . . [which] arises from our having one Father, One Saviour, and one indwelling Spirit."[6] In Eph 4:3–5, Paul calls the church to "[make] every effort to keep the unity of the Spirit." He made this appeal because the church is one body worshipping one God. The church has one Spirit, one Lord, and one God.

In 1 Corinthians 12, Paul made a similar appeal and observation. In this passage, he developed his famous body analogy, highlighting the importance of every gift, every ministry, and every member of the church.

> Indeed, the body is not one part but many. If the foot should say, "Because I'm not a hand, I don't belong to the body," it is not for that reason any less a part of the body. And if the ear should say, "Because I'm not an eye, I don't belong to the body," it is not for that reason any less a part of the body. If the whole body were an eye, where would the hearing be? If the whole body were an ear, where would the sense of smell be? But as it is, God has arranged each one of the parts in the body just

---

[6] John Stott, *The Message of Ephesians* (Downers Grove, IL: InterVarsity Press, 1979), 154.

as he wanted. And if they were all the same part, where would the body be? As it is, there are many parts, but one body. The eye cannot say to the hand, "I don't need you!" Or again, the head can't say to the feet, "I don't need you!" On the contrary, those parts of the body that are weaker are indispensable. And those parts of the body that we consider less honorable, we clothe these with greater honor, and our unrespectable parts are treated with greater respect, which our respectable parts do not need.

Instead, God has put the body together, giving greater honor to the less honorable, so that there would be no division in the body, but that the members would have the same concern for each other. (1 Cor 12:14–25)

The foundation of this illustration is Paul's claim that the ministry of the church is one cohesive effort because God is one. The ministry is given by the "same Spirit . . . the same Lord. And . . . the same God" (1 Cor 12:4–6).

In both passages, the unity of the church is rooted in the very nature of God. The appeal for unity within the body is first aimed at interpersonal relationships. However, the goal of this interpersonal unity is unity in ministry. Both Eph 4:11–13 and 1 Corinthians 12 portray unity as the foundation for local church ministry. Effective ministry in the church is made possible by unity of the body. The body is one because God is one. These verses demonstrate how our cooperative mission should be rooted in worship of our one God.

2. The Church Is Shaped by a Shared History and Future Hope

A second reason for unity and ministry partnership is the shared redemptive history of the church. In both passages, Paul reminds the churches they are one body through the gospel. In 1 Cor 12:12–13 he wrote, "For just as the body is one and has many parts, and all the parts of that body, though many, are one body—so also is Christ. For we were all baptized by one Spirit into one body." This allusion to baptism highlights that the church exists because of God's redemptive mission. The same point is made in Ephesians 4. Church unity is rooted in "one faith, one baptism" (v. 5). However, Paul added "one hope" (v. 4) to the list of unifying features. The church's common experience with the gospel includes both saving faith and future hope. The church ministers in the light of the return of Christ. This hope is the culmination of the gospel and an important basis for church unity and cooperation in mission.

This history and hope is not only a reason for unity. These phrases reveal a connection between God's mission and the ministry of the local church. The church exists through the redemptive work of Christ. Paul anchored the unity and ministry of the church in God's mission to redeem people from all nations. As the church engages in ministry/mission, we do so as the recipient and the agent of God's mission. When Southern Baptists consider cooperation between local churches, we must realize that we participate in one mission as one body. Cooperation should be the natural result of our redemptive history and future hope.

3. The Church Receives One Calling

These passages highlight that cooperation between local churches is more than a practical advantage. There are deeply theological reasons for pursuing cooperation in mission. Partnership in ministry is linked to the very nature of the church and its place in God's mission. Local churches, though autonomous, are not independent. Instead, they are interdependent, cooperating as members of the single universal church. Even though Southern Baptists rightly claim that cooperation allows us to do more together than we can separately, this pragmatic advantage should not be the foundational issue driving cooperation. For Southern Baptists, theological realities should encourage us to fully participate in the cooperative efforts of our convention. We are on mission together, not merely because it seems to work better, but because we are one church serving the same mission.

WHAT IS THE CHURCH TO DO?

What is the church to do as it seeks to fulfill God's mission of redemption and restoration? The mission of the church has been defined and described in many ways. At the end of the gospels of Matthew and Luke, and at the beginning of the book of Acts, we find key summary statements commonly referred to as *Great Commission texts*.[7]

When someone uses the phrase *Great Commission*, he or she probably has Matt 28:18–20 in mind. This passage is considered by many to be one of the most important missionary passages in the Bible. For evangelicals, the history of our missionary advance is linked to this passage. In 1792, William Carey used this passage as the biblical support in his famous missionary tract, *An Enquiry into the Obligation of Christians to Use Means for the Conversion of the Heathen*. Most missiologists agree that this booklet, along with Carey's missionary activity, gave birth to the modern

---

[7] Some form of the Great Commission is given in every gospel: Matt 28:18–20, Mark 16:15–18, Luke 24:44–49, John 20:21. A similar commission is found in Acts 1:8.

missionary movement. Yet Matthew 28 not only has historical importance. It is also important for theological purposes. It represents an important connection between the Old and New Testaments. According to Andreas Köstenberger and Peter O'Brien, the passage is not merely an addendum to the book. Rather, it is "intricately interwoven with the gospel as a whole."[8] These final verses of the first gospel can be understood as a summary of the book's overarching theme.

A similar observation can be made about Luke's Great Commission passages. According to missiologist David Bosch, "Jesus' words . . . reflect, in a nutshell, Luke's entire understanding of the Christian mission. . . . the fibers of Luke's mission theology."[9] Like Matthew's, Luke's writings are extremely important for understanding New Testament missiology. After all, Luke wrote nearly a quarter of the New Testament. It is safe to assume his ideas about the church's mission were influenced by his travels with the greatest missionary of the early church, the apostle Paul. What follows is an exploration of Great Commission tasks described by Luke and Matthew.

Preach and Witness

In Luke 24 and Acts 1, the church is assigned the task of proclaiming or preaching the gospel. Jesus told his disciples, "This is what is written: The Messiah would suffer and rise from the dead . . . and repentance for forgiveness of sins would be proclaimed in his name" (Luke 24:46–47). The mission of the church is to let the world know that Jesus died and rose again. The message of the church is that forgiveness of sins is available. Jesus reminded his disciples that God's mission was accomplished by the death and resurrection of Jesus. It will be advanced as Christians proclaim this message.

In both Luke and Acts, the apostles are called witnesses. In Luke 24:48 Jesus says of his disciples, "You are witnesses of these things." Then in Acts 1:8 he tells them that after the coming of the Holy Spirit, "you will be my witnesses in Jerusalem, in all Judea and Samaria, and to the end of the earth." The disciples had lived with Jesus. They heard his teachings, saw his miracles, and then experienced his betrayal, crucifixion, and resurrection. As witnesses, they were not to create their own message. Witnesses are only called upon to tell what they have personally experienced. The mission of the disciples as witnesses was to provide a verbal testimony of all God had done, and was doing, to save the lost and reach the nations. God loves the world, but sin has destroyed the relationship between God and his creation. Forgiveness of

[8] Andreas J. Köstenberger and Peter T. O'Brien, *Salvation to the Ends of the Earth: A Biblical Theology of Mission* (Downers Grove, IL: InterVarsity, 2001) 102.
[9] Bosch, *Transforming Mission*, 91.

sin has been made possible through the death and resurrection of Christ. Jesus has commissioned his followers to proclaim this to all people.

Make Disciples

In Matthew's gospel, the Great Commission commands followers of Jesus to "make disciples of all nations." According to Craig Blomberg, this command describes "a kind of evangelism that does not stop after someone makes a profession of faith. . . . [It is] a perennially incomplete lifelong task."[10] According to Matthew 28, followers of Jesus engage in disciple-making when we are "baptizing them in the name of the Father and of the Son and of the Holy Spirit" and are "teaching them to observe everything [Jesus has] commanded" (Matt 28:19). The mission of the church is sharing the gospel with the lost, planting churches (or connecting the new believer to a local church), and guiding new believers to grow in the faith. As this ongoing disciple-making mission happens, local churches reproduce themselves around the world.

Through these activities, followers of Jesus introduce those who are far away from God to him. According to one Bible scholar, making disciples "always implies the existence of a personal attachment which shapes the whole life."[11] Missionary anthropologist Paul Hiebert has developed a colorful, and accurate, description of the task of disciple-makers: "People are called to leave their false gods and their self-idolatry with its obsession with wealth, power, pride, sex, and race and to return to God as their creator and Lord. Real conversion involves real people in their real, everyday lives."[12] The church is God's means for accomplishing his mission, resaving fallen men and women.

To the Nations

One of the most striking aspects of the Great Commission is its far-reaching nature. The mission given to the church by Jesus encompasses the whole world and all people. Matthew's gospel says, "Go . . . make disciples of all nations" (Matt 28:19). Luke wrote of "repentance for forgiveness of sins . . . proclaimed in his name to all the nations" (Luke 24:47). Then in Acts 1:8, the disciples are commissioned to be witnesses "to the end of the earth." These phrases must have shocked the early church. Small bands of believers in backwater towns are called to a universal, global mission,

---

[10] Craig Blomberg, *Matthew*, NAC (Nashville: Broadman Press, 1992), 431.

[11] See μαθητής, in Gerhard Kittel, *TDNT* (Grand Rapids: Eerdmans, 1967), 4:441.

[12] Paul Hiebert, *Transforming Worldviews: An Anthropological Understanding of How People Change* (Grand Rapids: Baker Academic, 2008), 307.

a mission that extends beyond their experience or imagination. The commission is not only staggering in scope; it also carries significant theological and missiological meaning.

Both Matthew and Luke wrote their gospels to show Jesus was the Savior of the whole world, not just the chosen nation of Israel. As noted in chapter 4, even though God's mission was centered on one nation, Israel, it included all the nations. Jesus commissions his followers to embrace, and even participate in, this global movement—the mission of God. The boundaries of ministry have been eliminated, and the church is sent to all the world. The prophet Isaiah predicted the universal nature of God's mission:

> Isaiah 48:20
> Declare with a shout of joy, proclaim this, *let it go out to the end of the earth*; announce, "The LORD has redeemed his servant Jacob!" (emphasis added)

> Isaiah 49:6
> It is not enough for you to be my servant raising up the tribes of Jacob and restoring the protected ones of Israel. I will also make you *a light for the nations*, to be my *salvation to the ends of the earth.* (emphasis added)

God's mission has always included the whole world. Now the church has received a commission to join this global mission.

The Great Commission gives shape to the mission of the church, which is also God's mission. Every aspect of this work is carried out in the context of local churches. Cooperation among local churches is expected because a local church's mission is also the mission of every other local church. In the next chapter, we will look at how the early church practiced missions. We will see that from the birth of the church, missions was a joint venture. Southern Baptist cooperation has biblical support.

6

THE EARLY CHURCH AND ITS COOPERATIVE MISSION

T he New Testament church fully embraced a missionary identity. F. F. Bruce
    has observed how Christianity expanded far beyond its original context:
"Christianity arose as a movement within the Jewish community.... Yet in little more
than a generation.... [it] was recognized by the authorities of the Roman Empire
as a predominantly Gentile cult."[1] Though much of the credit for this missionary
advance has been given to Paul and his missionary team, the New Testament does
not portray it as the work of a single church or independent missionary team.
Rather, at every turn, the missionary expansion of the early church was a partnership
between sending/mother churches, newly planted/daughter churches, and the sent-
out missionary team. An overlooked New Testament fact is that Paul's missionary
travels, in large part, are portrayed as the missionary extension of several local
churches.

THE MISSION EXPANDS TO THE GENTILES

Acts 11 is a turning point in the story of early Christian missions. In this chapter, the
leaders of the church in Jerusalem call Peter to meet with them to explain why he had
eaten with Gentiles. He responded by describing a vision he had received, recorded
in Acts 10. His obedience to God's command in that vision led to the conversion of,
and outpouring of the Holy Spirit on, Cornelius and his household. When Peter's
critics heard the story, they broke into spontaneous worship and declared, "God
has given repentance resulting in life even to the Gentiles" (Acts 11:18). The phrase
"even to the Gentiles" signals a shift of emphasis in the book of Acts. The remainder
of the book describes the church's mission to the ends of the earth. The church in

---

[1] F. F. Bruce, *Paul: Apostle of the Heart Set Free* (Grand Rapids: Eerdmans, 1977) 17.

Jerusalem realized that the gospel was good news for all people, in all places, regardless of ethnic and cultural differences.

As previously noted, in Acts 1:8, Jesus promised that the gospel would reach the ends of the earth. However, until chapter 11, evangelism of Jews is the book's main focus. This story is the beginning of a new phase in the missionary vision of the church; they publicly embrace the Gentile mission and begin sending cross-cultural missionaries.

The Gentile mission begins with the planting in Antioch of the first church composed primarily of Gentiles. Luke records the event in Acts 11:19–21:

> Now those who had been scattered as a result of the persecution that started because of Stephen made their way as far as Phoenicia, Cyprus, and Antioch, speaking the word to no one except Jews. But there were some of them, men from Cyprus and Cyrene, who came to Antioch and began speaking to the Greeks also, proclaiming the good news about the Lord Jesus. The Lord's hand was with them, and a large number who believed turned to the Lord.

Köstenberger and O'Brien claim this church plant was, "in one sense the most important in the history of Christian mission."[2] This new church soon became a powerful missionary-sending church, and for all intents and purposes, the course of both Christian and missions history changed.

When the church in Jerusalem heard that a large number of Gentiles were coming to faith, they sent Barnabas to Antioch. Some have interpreted this negatively, as if the Jerusalem Christians sought to control the situation. However, it is probably better to understand the church's action as sending Barnabas in a missionary capacity. Although the term *missionary* is not used to describe the visit, Barnabas's work seems to fit the label. First, he "encouraged all of them to remain true" (Acts 11:23). Second, he apparently engaged in evangelism, because Luke connects his visit with the fact that "large numbers of people were added to the Lord" (Acts 11:24). Third, Barnabas built a missionary team by seeking and then bringing Saul (Paul) to work with him in the church (Acts 11:25–26). Barnabas crossed into a different culture to evangelize, disciple, and develop local leaders. In other words, he engaged in activities that most people associate with the term *missionary*. By sending Barnabas as a missionary, the church in Jerusalem helped establish the church in Antioch.

---

[2] Köstenberger and O'Brien, *Salvation to the Ends of the Earth*, 145 (see chap. 5, n. 8).

THE MISSION BECOMES A COOPERATIVE EFFORT

The next phase of the early church's mission began in Acts 11:27 when the Antioch church received word that their brothers in Jerusalem were suffering. In response to this word, they decided to send Barnabas and Paul with a financial gift. This is a significant event for two reasons. First, it shows the young church had developed an independent identity and embraced a missionary vision to minister cross-culturally. Second, during his visit to Jerusalem, Paul had an important missionary strategy meeting that shaped his calling and future ministry. In Galatians 2, Paul recorded details of this high-level missionary consultation in Jerusalem.

> Now from those recognized as important (what they once were makes no difference to me; God does not show favoritism)—they added nothing to me. On the contrary, they saw that I had been entrusted with the gospel for the uncircumcised, just as Peter was for the circumcised, since the one at work in Peter for an apostleship to the circumcised was also at work in me for the Gentiles. When James, Cephas, and John—those recognized as pillars—acknowledged the grace that had been given to me, they gave the right hand of fellowship to me and Barnabas, agreeing that *we should go to the Gentiles and they to the circumcised.* They asked only that we would remember the poor, which I had made every effort to do. (Gal 2:6–10, emphasis added)

During this meeting, the leaders of the Jerusalem church affirmed Paul's message and agreed on a missionary strategy. Paul and Barnabas were sent to the Gentiles while Peter and the Jerusalem church leadership would continue working among the Jews. It is difficult to overstate the importance of this meeting as it relates to the mission of the early church.

According to Gal 2:2, Paul initiated the conversation "to be sure I was not running, and had not been running, in vain." Paul was not a new convert. In fact, he had been in ministry for 14 years (see Gal 2:1), so it is inconceivable that he was worried about the content of his preaching. Instead, he seems to have been concerned about the sustainability of his missionary efforts. F. F. Bruce has rightly noted that

> what Paul was concerned about was not the validity of his gospel but its practicability. His commission was not derived from Jerusalem, but it could not be effectively discharged except in fellowship with Jerusalem. A cleavage between his Gentile mission and the mother-church in Jerusalem would be disastrous for the progress of the gospel.[3]

---

[3] Bruce, *Paul: Apostle of the Heart Set Free*, 152.

He wanted to ensure that the missionary efforts of the early churches were in concert, not competition. Paul did not view himself as an independent missionary. Rather, he seems to have understood his ministry as a collaborative, or even cooperative, endeavor. Paul and Barnabas had been sent out by the Antioch church. Now, they sought advice and endorsement from the Jerusalem church.

From the earliest days of Christian missions, missionary teams operated with some degree of accountability to both major churches of their day: Jerusalem and Antioch. Even though the Bible does not record examples of consultation between the two churches, the New Testament pictures their missionary advance as the work of both churches. Their mission is God's mission, and because of this, they worked together.

The story of the New Testament church's mission continues in Acts 13:

> Now in the church at Antioch there were prophets and teachers: Barnabas, Simeon who was called Niger, Lucius of Cyrene, Manaen, a close friend of Herod the tetrarch, and Saul.

> As they were worshiping the Lord and fasting, the Holy Spirit said, "Set apart for me Barnabas and Saul for the work to which I have called them." Then after they had fasted, prayed, and laid hands on them, they sent them off. (vv. 1–3)

New Testament scholar Darrell Bock calls this "the first steps in 'missions' as the called-out and divinely directed activity of a group organized for this specific goal. This contrasts with the less-systematic work of individuals mentioned earlier. The church is becoming more organized and intentional about outreach."[4] In Acts 13, the Antioch church accepts the role of appointing and sending out Paul and Barnabas as a missionary team. The picture in this chapter is of different local churches sharing responsibility for the same missionary team.[5]

Though there isn't any explicit record of the churches communicating with each other about missions, Luke shows autonomous churches cooperating in the mission. The churches participated in the sending and shaping of Paul's missionary strategy: Jerusalem provided strategic consultation, and Antioch affirmed this by sending them to preach to the Gentiles. Those who denounce cooperation among churches lack New Testament support for their position. In fact, even newly planted churches served as partners in the missionary advance.

---

[4] Darryl L. Bock, *Acts*, BECNT (Grand Rapids: Baker Academic, 2007), 437.

[5] Another bit of evidence that supports the idea of cooperation can be noted by the inclusion of John Mark, the author of the second gospel. He was an important member in the Jerusalem church, and he joined Paul and Barnabas on this missionary tour for a time before returning to the Jerusalem church (Acts 13:5, 13).

Daughter Churches Join the Mission

The New Testament clearly portrays multiple churches supporting and sharing in the missionary advance. Daughter churches, like their parent congregations in Jerusalem and Antioch, supported missions in several ways.

Finances

Almost any time someone thinks about cooperation in missions, the primary emphasis is financial. The New Testament does not shy away from this topic. Though there were times Paul refused financial assistance from churches (e.g., 1 Thess 2:7–9), the New Testament contains clear evidence of multiple churches jointly supporting his missionary work financially. For example, at the conclusion of his letter to the Romans, Paul wrote, "For I hope to see you when I pass through and to be assisted by you for my journey" (Rom 15:24). Robert Mounce has noted that the phrase "to be assisted by you" carries the idea of receiving spiritual as well as material help from this young church.[6] Paul let the Christians in Rome know he was planning to visit them on his way to Spain and that their financial support was necessary for the success of the next phase of missionary advance.

A second example of financial assistance being provided by a fledgling church can be seen in Paul's letter to the Philippians. In the opening verses of the letter, he thanked the church for their "partnership in the gospel from the first day until now" (Phil 1:5). Then, at the conclusion of the letter, he thanked the church again for their financial support (Phil 4:15–20). The church in Philippi was planted as a direct result of Paul's missionary work (see Acts 16). Through financial gifts, they became a partner in the mission of proclaiming the gospel to the unreached.

Prayer

A second way newly planted churches cooperated in missions was through prayer. In almost all of Paul's letters, he reminded the churches he was praying for them. There are other instances when Paul requested prayer for himself and the mission.

> Now I appeal to you, brothers and sisters, through our Lord Jesus Christ and through the love of the Spirit, to strive together with me in fervent prayers to God on my behalf. Pray that I may be rescued from the unbelievers in Judea, that my ministry to Jerusalem may be

---

[6] Robert Mounce, *Romans*, NAC (Nashville: Broadman and Holman, 1995), 269.

> acceptable to the saints, and that, by God's will, I may come to you with joy and be refreshed together with you. (Rom 15:30–32)

And,

> In addition, brothers and sisters, pray for us that the word of the Lord may spread rapidly and be honored, just as it was with you, and that we may be delivered from wicked and evil people, for not all have faith. (2 Thess 3:1–2)

In both of these passages, Paul requested prayer as a means of missionary support. Through prayer, these new churches served as partners in the mission.

Even though Paul was a seasoned missionary, he realized success depended on God's blessing. He also knew the mission of the church required every church to participate. Through prayer, new believers and churches partnered together for the sake of God's mission. Leon Morris has observed:

> It is easy to picture for ourselves Paul as a very great apostle ceaselessly occupied with his work of issuing directives to other people on how they should live out their faith, while he himself sits above the storm or calmly proceeds along on his undisturbed way. Such, of course, is far from being a true picture. . . . He was very conscious of his own limitations and knew that his only hope was in God. So quite often we find him seeking the prayers of his converts.[7]

Paul was not asking prayer merely for himself; his concern was for the advancement of the gospel. These young churches were partners in ministry, and they shared in the support of the missionary advance with other churches. While there is no direct assertion in Scripture of official collaborative prayer campaigns, the New Testament suggests the early church understood its mission was to be accomplished cooperatively.

Building Missionary Teams

One other way newly planted churches partnered together was in supplying workers for the missionary team.

- Epaphroditus was sent from the Philippian church with a financial gift, and he eventually became Paul's "brother, coworker, and fellow soldier" (Phil 2:25; see also 4:18).

---

[7] Leon Morris, *1–2 Thessalonians*, NICNT (Grand Rapids: Eerdmans, 1991), 184–95.

- Epaphras came from Colossae and joined Paul's missionary team to become a "fellow prisoner in Christ Jesus" and a "faithful minister of Christ on [the Colossian church's] behalf" (Phlm 1:23; Col 1:7; see also Col 4:12).
- Aristarchus joined Paul from Thessalonica and continued to minister alongside him as they traveled to Macedonia. He was later imprisoned on a ship with Paul as they journeyed to Rome. In Paul's letters to Philemon and the church at Colossae, Aristarchus is introduced as "a fellow prisoner" and "coworker" (Acts 19:29; 20:4; 27:2; Phlm 1:24; Col 4:10).

Each of these men made a significant contribution to the mission. One might assume new church plants need to keep all available mature believers in the church. In these young churches, however, this was not the assumption. These churches understood that the mission demanded joint participation. In response, they sent missionaries to join the team. Missiologist David Bosch has written that through these coworkers, "the churches . . . identify with [Paul's] missionary efforts; this is the primary intention of the cooperative missions."[8]

Just like the sending churches, church plants served as significant partners in the New Testament missionary program. Their cooperation was a necessary component of missional success. Some might argue such cooperation took place solely out of necessity; there was too much to do for such small communities of faith to go it alone. This may be true. Taking the gospel to the ends of the earth was surely a daunting commission for these fledgling churches. However, there is no place in the New Testament where cooperation is recommended as an unusual measure only for extraordinary times. Instead, cooperation is portrayed as a normal component of God's mission.

When Southern Baptists think about our cooperative structure and the Cooperative Program, it is easy to explain the benefits pragmatically. However, when we reduce the benefit of cooperation to merely "doing more together than we can do apart," we miss key theological and biblical teachings. The New Testament church did not create a Cooperative Program. The churches were not organized in a complex structure like the SBC. However, our study of the New Testament has shown that their mode of missions was cooperative. When Southern Baptists participate in the cooperative ministries of the convention, we are following a pattern established in the Bible. It is not necessary to find a one-to-one correlation between Scripture and the structures and mechanisms of the convention. Structures and mechanisms must change and adapt to the needs of the day. Yet when we consider abandoning cooperation because it is difficult or uncomfortable, we need to understand that this attitude cannot be justified biblically.

---

[8] Bosch, *Transforming Mission*, 132 (see chap. 4, n. 5).

Part III

Southern Baptists: A People Pursuing God's Mission

The preceding chapters have prepared the way for what follows. We have looked at the history of the Southern Baptist Convention. Southern Baptists have made strategic decisions contributing to a unique denominational identity. As Baptists, we believe in the autonomy and sufficiency of the local church. As Southern Baptists, we also believe these convictions do not mandate independence. Rather, we fully embrace the idea that God's will for us mandates working together. Cooperation is our denominational identity.

Cooperation is more than a programmatic value. As we have seen, cooperation between churches fits perfectly with God's intention for his people. Local Southern Baptist churches, though completely autonomous, are commissioned to participate in God's global mission. We worship one God with one mission. Each local church is not permitted to create its own mission. Thus, cooperation is not merely pragmatic or programmatic. It is fundamental to full participation in God's mission.

The previous chapters have helped shine light on the current state of our convention. In the pages to follow, I will propose a renewed vision and definition for Southern Baptist cooperation. I will also attempt to show how different SBC entities fit within God's mission and how, by cooperating, local Southern Baptist churches, regardless of size, can more fully engage in this mission. This book is intended to be an optimistic one. Sure, the Southern Baptist Convention is not perfect. We have troubles within and face external challenges as well. However, my conclusion is that of all denominations in the world, Southern Baptists, because of our heritage and structure, are most capable of pursuing God's mission. And Southern Baptist churches, by virtue of our cooperative structure, are able to fully embrace God's mission.

7

A Proposal for Southern Baptist Cooperation

The History of Southern Baptist Cooperation

The founding of the Southern Baptist Convention is marred by its connection to slavery. However, it is a mistake to reduce its birth to a single issue. In 1845, when Southern Baptists separated from the Triennial Convention, the founders of the SBC gathered for the purpose of "eliciting, combining and directing the energies of the whole denomination in one sacred effort, for the propagation of the Gospel." This statement signaled an intentional departure from the mission society structure of the Triennial Convention and moved Southern Baptists toward a more robust convention encouraging churches to voluntarily cooperate in support of multiple denominational ministries.

Southern Baptists did not immediately break from the funding practices of mission societies. However, the Seventy-Five Million Campaign was a watershed event in Southern Baptist history. For the first time, churches were encouraged to develop a stewardship plan and send regular offerings to the convention. The campaign ended with mixed results. On one hand, churches failed to fulfill pledges, leaving the convention on the brink of bankruptcy. However, the $58,591,713 collected was more than the convention had previously raised in a financial campaign. Southern Baptists learned that working together allowed them to achieve more than their previous independent efforts.

The Seventy-Five Million Campaign paved the way for two of the most significant actions the convention has ever taken related to cooperation, actions that galvanized the Southern Baptist Convention as a cooperative body. For Southern Baptists, cooperation came to mean more than supporting convention initiatives. Lack of cooperation was interpreted as a spiritual deficit.

In 1925, Southern Baptists established the Cooperative Program. This unified budget supports all of the convention's efforts—missions, education, publication, and so on. Southern Baptist churches are encouraged to set aside and send a percentage of their receipts to their respective state conventions. State conventions then use a portion of these monies to support state mission causes and send the remainder to the Executive Committee in Nashville for support of wider Southern Baptist Convention ministries. The Cooperative Program is both the chief funding source and lifeline for the growth of the convention. It shapes our identity as a cooperative body.

Along with the Cooperative Program, in 1925 Southern Baptists adopted a statement of faith, the Baptist Faith and Message. Among the reasons this statement was adopted was to confront concerns about the teaching of evolution in Baptist colleges. This statement also formalized cooperation as a theological doctrine, reacting to the anti-denominational rhetoric of fundamentalism. The establishment of the Cooperative Program and the inclusion of this doctrine in the Baptist Faith and Message indicated the importance of cooperation to the identity of the Southern Baptist Convention.

Since 1925, Southern Baptists have endured several denominational skirmishes. During these times of tension, some questioned the wisdom of cooperating with those with whom they disagreed. Yet, by and large, Southern Baptists have not seriously questioned cooperation as a valuable denominational goal. At the end of the twentieth century, Southern Baptists underwent a significant reorganization. Several convention entities were eliminated, and others had their duties adjusted. The goal of this reorganization was efficiency and reaffirmation of cooperation as a key component of Southern Baptist identity.

THEOLOGY FOR SOUTHERN BAPTIST COOPERATION

Often Southern Baptists promote cooperation without offering a theological support for their practice. One will look in vain for a specific Bible verse calling for support of the Cooperative Program. Yet Scripture does present a theological framework that includes cooperation between churches.

The Bible tells the story of a God on mission. He created the world and declared it "very good" (Gen 1:31). As discussed in chapter 4, because of human rebellion, we no longer live in a very good world. Human sin has corrupted this world, and we live among a fallen people. Humanity rejected God's law and now lives under the penalty of sin. Because of God's love for the world, he is on mission to rescue and redeem his fallen creation.

Throughout the Bible God uses people to advance his mission. In the Old Testament, God chose Israel to be a kingdom of priests and a light to the nations. But the nation failed repeatedly. Rather than embracing God's mission, Israel abandoned his truth and ended up exiled to foreign lands.

In the New Testament, God's mission has been entrusted to the church. Jesus commissioned the church to proclaim the gospel and make disciples of all people groups, to the ends of the earth. This mission belongs to the universal church and to each local church. The story of the New Testament church shows us that first-generation Christians embraced their role in God's mission. They received a commission through their one Lord. And though different local churches were spread out across Asia, they engaged in a single mission together.

Some have asserted that traditional Baptist belief in the authority and autonomy of the local church is a strike against cooperation. As the argument goes, cooperation wrongly requires individual churches to give up some independence in favor of a shared vision. Such claims cannot be supported adequately. For Southern Baptists, there is a solid biblical basis for our cooperative vision. It is true that Southern Baptist churches can achieve more when we cooperate than we could separately. However, this should not be the primary basis for cooperation. If we focus on productivity alone, it is tempting to find an easier, less complicated path. Yet, if we allow the scriptural vision to shape our understanding of our church's mission, we will see that cooperation is biblical. Are there challenges associated with our current structure and mechanisms of cooperation? Most certainly. Still, independence should not be viewed as the noble path forward. With Scripture as our guide, we can see the need to embrace cooperation as the means of Southern Baptist missions.

COOPERATIVE PROGRAM TODAY

Through the years, the Cooperative Program has been a source of funding and convention identity. It has also served as a unifying factor for Southern Baptists and continues to generate more than $400 million annually for missions and ministries within state conventions and the SBC. However, the percentage of churches' receipts forwarded through the CP has declined significantly over the past several decades.[1]

---

[1] Historically the Annual Church Profile (ACP), formally Uniform Church Letter, has provided a reliable "trend line" of various church-related metrics for Southern Baptists. For example, through the ACP, churches self-report missions giving, baptisms, and (since 1982) undesignated receipts. This report is voluntary, and each year many thousands of SBC churches report $0.00 missions' gifts/contributions or they provide no ACP report at all.

As we seek to understand the financial support of Southern Baptist missions and ministries through the Cooperative Program, we must remember that when LifeWay Research reports the average Cooperative Program gift per church, as a percentage of the church's undesignated receipts, the computation includes upwards of 10,000 churches reporting $0.00 missions' gifts/contributions of any kind on their ACP report.

The "official" Cooperative Program contributions are independent of the ACP because these numbers are reported and accounted for by the state conventions. Generally speaking, the "official" SBC Annual, yearly printed and published, as well as online at www.sbc.net, is the gold standard of statistical reporting.

Brand and Hankins observe, "From the early 1930s until the mid–1980s, gifts to the Cooperative Program grew from $2,421,118 to $325,436,882. The percentage of churches' aggregate undesignated receipts given through the Cooperative Program was consistently in the 10.5 to 11 percent range."[2] Between 1978 and 2008, however, the average percentage of churches' total gifts channeled through the CP fell 45 percent, from 8.83 percent to 4.88 percent. Between 1998 and 2008 it fell 23 percent (from 6.36 percent to 4.88 percent).[3] This decline is starker when one realizes that 2007–08 stands as the high-water mark for contributions to Southern Baptist churches. That fiscal year, Southern Baptists gave more than $12 billion to their respective churches. To be fair, 2008 also marked the high point of CP income, at $548,205,099.[4] In the fiscal year 2015, the average percentage increased to 5.18 percent; however, the trend of Southern Baptist churches choosing to give a decreased percentage of their receipts to denominational cooperative causes continues.

From the establishment of the Cooperative Program, churches have been encouraged to set aside a percentage of regular receipts as a CP contribution. Brand and Hankins noted, "For decades, the regular increase in a church's Cooperative Program percentage was promoted as a virtue and was a sign of a healthy Southern Baptist congregation. . . . However, the percentage . . . contributed through the Cooperative Program began serious decline in 1985. . . . From 1984 to 2004 [it] declined from 10.6% to 6.99%"[5] According to LifeWay Research's report on Cooperative Giving from 2007 to 2011,[6] in 2011 only 9 percent of reporting churches gave 10 percent of undesignated receipts through the Cooperative Program. The average percentage given was 4.58 percent.

One might assume these statistics indicate a lack of appreciation or unfavorable attitude toward the Cooperative Program. But this is not the case. LifeWay Research has reported that the vast majority of Southern Baptists expressed positive feelings about the Cooperative Program. "When forced to indicate if they are generally satisfied or dissatisfied with the CP, 87% of pastors and more than 90% of other ministers and laity indicated they are generally satisfied."[7] One major reason for this level of satisfaction is the conviction that the Cooperative Program increases a church's ability to participate effectively in missionary endeavors. Southern Baptists value the opportunity to cooperate with others rather than do missions alone. The majority of those surveyed (64 percent of pastors, 60 percent of other ministers, and 56 percent

---

[2] Brand and Hankins, *One Sacred Effort*, 160 (see chap. 3, n. 7).

[3] Data compiled from SBC Annuals by the SBC Executive Committee. Past SBC Annuals can be accessed at http://www.sbcec.org or www.sbc.net.

[4] Shawn Hendricks, "Hunt, Rankin Urge Baptists to Reprioritize," *Baptist News*, May 21, 2009, http://www.bpnews.net/30536/hunt-rankin-urge-baptists-to-reprioritize.

[5] Brand and Owen, *One Sacred Effort*, 160–61.

[6] LifeWay Research, "CP Giving as Reported in the Annual Church Profile 2007–2011."

[7] LifeWay Research, "Cooperative Program and Stewardship: A Census of Southern Baptist Pastors and Selected Laity," PowerPoint presentation, 6.

of lay leaders) strongly agreed that the Cooperative Program was the *most effective* and efficient way to support the spread of the gospel worldwide. These statistics indicate that Southern Baptists, regardless of their roles in the local church, believe the Cooperative Program is an important tool to facilitate missions.

The Cooperative Program's struggles are real. In 2016, in order to address major budget issues, the International Mission Board reduced its overseas force. Nearly 1,000 international missionaries left the mission field and returned to America.[8] Staff cuts also have taken place at the NAMB and other Cooperative Program entities. Frank Page, former president of the SBC Executive Committee, summed up the reaction of many when he said, "My heart is broken to hear of the large number of missionaries and staff who are leaving the IMB. My prayers are with them as they transition. However most of all, my prayers are focused on the fact of the massive lostness in our world."[9] Obviously, staff reductions at SBC entities cannot be reduced to inadequate CP giving. Other factors were at work. Still, more giving through CP may have allowed the IMB and other entities to keep personnel on the field.

Thankfully, Southern Baptists remain committed to missions and cooperation. Following are several recommendations to help Southern Baptists understand and commit to our convention's mission and cooperative vision.

A WAY FORWARD

Southern Baptists are facing several obstacles that threaten to undermine our cooperative mission. We are in the midst of what some might call a generational "changing of the guard." For the past three or four decades, the Southern Baptist Convention has been led by men who were linked to the Conservative Resurgence. Recently, a new, younger group of leaders has begun emerging. These leaders are heirs of the Conservative Resurgence, but they have no direct connection. This generational change is creating tension in the convention. Younger Southern Baptists express themselves differently, have different priorities, and request changes in the convention. These pressure points are not surprising. Our future will always include generational issues such as those we are currently experiencing.

Though Southern Baptists are committed to a common statement of faith, the Baptist Faith and Message, theological controversies around the doctrine of salvation also are creating tension in the convention. Baptist history shows we are the heirs of different soteriological traditions. Some Southern Baptists have chosen to make these traditions a basis of fellowship. Some are embracing a label of "Reformed" and others "Traditionalist." As with the tensions created by generational

---

[8] See BP Staff, "IMB: 1,132 Missionaries, Staff Accept VRI, HRO," *Baptist Press*, February 2, 2016, http://www.bpnews.net/46374/imb-1132-missionaries-staff-accept-vri-hro.
[9] Ibid.

changes, we should anticipate there will be disagreements on these issues. It is naive to believe a body as large as the Southern Baptist Convention will be able to settle a debate that has been raging for hundreds of years. While theological convictions are indeed necessary, it is important for Southern Baptists to seek unity under our common statement of faith and around our common cooperative vision. We cannot make cooperation dependent upon the absence of theological debate.

Southern Baptists must embrace a vision and understanding of cooperation that does not rely on bureaucratic structures, and that is more robust than mere financial contribution to convention causes. Of course, the Southern Baptist Convention needs organization, financial contributions, and even to develop convention-wide strategies. However, each of these must be sustained by biblical and theological reflection.

Understanding what the Bible teaches about God's mission can help us. The Bible tells the story of one God with one mission. This mission leads to the establishment of a people, the one church, sent together to the nations. Local churches should participate in the mission of this one God. It is within this framework that cooperation among local congregations takes place. Keeping these points in mind, a helpful understanding of cooperation for Southern Baptists might be:

> Local churches voluntarily choosing to join with other local churches as an expression of the oneness of the church and as a means of fully participating in the single mission of God as he works through his people to redeem the nations and restore the creation from the effects of the fall.

This definition positions Southern Baptist cooperation within the overall mission of God. It maintains the all-important Baptist doctrine of local church autonomy and avoids pragmatic and bureaucratic trappings.

RECOMMENDATIONS FOR COOPERATION

My purpose is not to recommend structural changes to the Southern Baptist Convention, or to the way Cooperative Program funds are dispersed. The goal here is to present a positive vision for cooperation. Each new generation of Southern Baptists will face challenges and opportunities unique to their day. My hope is that as we learn to promote cooperation biblically, we will be ready to embrace whatever God sends our way.

1. Let's Discuss Cooperation Theologically, not Structurally or Pragmatically

A concerning statistic from a 2012 LifeWay Research survey of Southern Baptist pastors related to Cooperative Program giving. Four out of five pastors (81 percent) reported they planned to keep church contributions though CP the same as the previous year. This finding came despite a strong appeal in 2012 by the Executive Committee for Southern Baptist churches to increase Cooperative Program giving by 1 percent of undesignated receipts. Of the pastors surveyed, 38 percent said they had not heard anything about the "1% Challenge"; 42 percent said they had heard of it but had no plans to accept it. Seven percent said they had taken the 1% Challenge, and data from the 2012 Annual Church Profile confirmed that.[10] On a more encouraging note, an estimated 24 percent of Southern Baptist churches had taken the 1% Challenge by 2015.[11] Still, a majority had not. In other words, even though Southern Baptist pastors are generally in favor of the Cooperative Program, by and large, appeals to increase giving do not appear to motivate action.

Whereas Southern Baptists have demonstrated that we can rise and meet immediate financial challenges, these statistics show that calls to "sacrifice and give more" are not sustainable over the long haul. On the other hand, Southern Baptists can be mobilized when a compelling theological vision is placed before us. The Conservative Resurgence not only proves this; it has given rise to a generation of younger Southern Baptists for whom theology serves as a greater motivational factor than tradition or denominational loyalty. Southern Baptist leaders need to demonstrate how our convention ministries, our cooperative identity, and the Cooperative Program serve to advance a biblical understanding of God's mission.

2. Let's Not Base the Label "Cooperating Churches" Exclusively on Financial Contributions

One of the issues we face as Southern Baptists is that we use the term *cooperation* without an agreed-upon definition or understanding. Article III of the SBC Constitution defines a church as being "in friendly cooperation with the Convention" if it "closely identifies with the Convention's adopted statement of faith," "has formally approved its intention to cooperate with the Southern Baptist Convention," and "has made undesignated, financial contribution(s) through the Cooperative Program, and/or through the Convention's Executive Committee for Convention causes, and/or to any Convention entity during the fiscal year preceding." Still, some Southern Baptists appear not to embrace this robust definition. Rather, they seem to limit cooperation to financial contribution through the Cooperative Program. I have tried to show that this understanding is too narrow. The definition I provided earlier explains cooperation as local churches "joining together . . . as a means of fully

---

[10] Staff/SBC LIFE, "1% CP Challenge: Learn, Pray, Give," Baptist Press, October 6, 2014, http://www.bpnews.net/43485/1-cp-challenge-learn-pray-give.

[11] Data compiled by the SBC Executive Committee based on Annual Church Profile reports.

participating in the mission of God." If the only thing many Southern Baptists hear when we say, "cooperation" is "giving money," something is wrong.

In addition to financial support through the Cooperative Program, consider some of the many ways Southern Baptist churches cooperate. A Southern Baptist church is cooperative when

- it sends a short-term mission team to serve alongside an International Mission Board missionary who was sent out by a different local church and is supported by our convention of churches
- it mobilizes members to work with a church plant in North America or serves a role in the revitalization of a church in a struggling area
- its members work alongside members of other Southern Baptist churches as part of disaster relief teams, to adopt a local school, or to engage in local community outreach
- it receives college or seminary students as a stewardship from their home churches; as these students mature and sense God's call to ministry, the mission field, or a professional career, both churches can celebrate the fruit of discipleship
- it hires a seminary student and patiently grooms him for service in another church or on the mission field
- it partners with other local churches to fulfill strategic association or state convention initiatives
- it utilizes its people and resources to partner with other local churches in engaging and planting churches among various people groups locally, nationally, or globally
- it empowers other ethno-linguistic people groups to plant new Southern Baptist churches that effectively reach that group
- it strategically works with other local churches to reach, engage, and minister within their community
- it seeks opportunities to partner with other churches to train and equip their members for ministry

Consider what a difference it might make in our convention if, when we asked about the cooperative investment of a church, we meant more than, "What percentage of your budget do you give through the Cooperative Program?" However, Dr Paul Chitwood, executive director-treasurer of the Kentucky Baptist Convention, has accurately and wisely observed that Southern Baptist cooperation does not mean zero financial contribution to our cooperative efforts, but it indeed means more than CP percentages.

3. Let's Advocate for the Cooperative Program as a Tool, Not a Tax

The Cooperative Program is a genius tool! It supports our theological convictions while providing financial resources for our mission boards and other entities. It is the financial driving force for the success and advance of our convention. Some Southern Baptists, however, seem to have a skewed understanding of the program. I have heard the Cooperative Program discussed as if it were a denominational tax or membership dues. It was never designed to be that, and these ideas reflect an unfortunate misunderstanding. This attitude creates bitterness and a sense of entitlement, and might tempt some to look for ways to avoid giving altogether.

Rather than taking a dim, perhaps even begrudging, attitude toward our Cooperative Program, let's advocate for it as a positive means for advancing God's kingdom. The Cooperative Program is the financial tool *through which* Southern Baptist churches partner in God's mission. I have already made a plea that we regard cooperation as including more than financial giving. But no one should be naive enough to believe we can send and support missionaries, church planters, seminary students, disaster relief projects, and so forth without a high level of financial investment. Imagine the joy a local church might experience if its members were to embrace the Cooperative Program as a means for fulfilling God's mission. I regularly tell churches that through their Cooperative Program gifts, their church has a ministry that is reaching the whole world. There is great celebration when a church cuts the ribbon on a new building because they see how their personal sacrifice has advanced the ministry of the church. Can we advocate the Cooperative Program with similar excitement?

CONCLUSION

I started this book by noting that I am a Southern Baptist writing to Southern Baptists. I know our convention is not perfect. If statistics are to be trusted, there are approximately 15 million reasons for our imperfection. I am one and so are you. Fellow Southern Baptists say things I disagree with. Some spend money on things I don't like. Some make decisions I think are foolish. Some Southern Baptists behave in ways I find offensive or embarrassing. But none of these realities can shake my desire to remain a Southern Baptist.

Now, some of you reading this book are not convinced. I hear regularly from younger men and women about frustrations and the temptation to leave the SBC for another denomination or independence. I find this sad. I hope you have seen through this book that our cooperation is more than a financial contribution. It is not merely a traditional way of doing things; it is a means for achieving God's global vision. We will hit bumps along the way, but I believe the Southern Baptist

Convention is uniquely structured and positioned to make a huge contribution to God's mission. Join me and other Southern Baptists so that, together, we can cooperate to fulfill the Great Commission for God's glory and the good of the nations.

STUDY QUESTIONS

Chapter 1

1. How was the Triennial Convention established?
2. What are the key differences between society and convention structure?
3. What four reasons were given for Baptists in the South being willing to embrace convention structure?
4. What role did Adoniram Judson, Luther Rice, Richard Furman, and W. B. Johnson play in the establishment of the Southern Baptist Convention?

Chapter 2

1. Why is the Seventy-Five Million Campaign considered a watershed event in Southern Baptist history?
2. What two events took place in 1925 that established "cooperation" as a key part of SBC identity?
3. What role did the fundamentalist/modernist controversy play in the content of the Baptist Faith and Message?

Chapter 3

1. How does the Cooperative Program fit within the Baptist affirmation of local church authority?
2. What is the typical flow of funds to, and through, the Cooperative Program?
3. How does a State Convention decide the percentage of Cooperative Program funds to keep and send to the Southern Baptist Convention?
4. How have recent changes in the SBC affected Cooperative Program funding and specific SBC entities?
5. Which SBC entities receive support through the Cooperative Program? Which SBC entities do not receive CP funding?

6. Briefly discuss the ministry responsibilities of these SBC entities.

Introduction to Part II

1. What is meant by the statement "Southern Baptists are *people of the Book*"?
2. Define *inerrancy*.
3. What does the phrase "autonomy of the local church" mean?

Chapter 4

1. What important elements of God's mission are revealed in the first three chapters of the Bible?
2. What are key differences between Israel and the church as God's missionary people?
3. What is meant by the phrase "one sacred effort"?

Chapter 5

1. Define *universal church* and *local church*.
2. How does the nature of the church encourage cooperation in mission?
3. Discuss the different components of the mission of the church as revealed through the Great Commission texts in Matthew and Luke/Acts.

Chapter 6

1. Discuss the cooperative contributions of the churches in Jerusalem and Antioch to the missionary advancements of the New Testament.
2. Why is Acts 13 a key text for cross-cultural missions?
3. Discuss the important cooperative role of daughter, or church plants, in the missionary advancement of the New Testament.

Chapter 7

1. Present a biblical/theological basis for cooperation.
2. Why is it important to develop a biblical/theological reason for cooperation?

3 What is the preferred definition, or description, of Southern Baptist cooperation presented in this chapter?

4. How can the Cooperative Program support Southern Baptist cooperation?

5. What suggestions would you make for understanding and advancing cooperation as a denomination and support of the Cooperative Program?

Name Index

A

Akin, Daniel   *31, 40, 57*

Ashford, Bruce   *57*

B

Baker, Robert A.   *13, 19*

Ball, Rev. M.   *15*

Barnes, William Wright   *8, 12*

Berntson, Ben   *17*

Blomberg, Craig   *62*

Blount, Douglas   *44, 46–47*

Bock, Darryl L.   *68*

Bosch, David   *52, 61, 71*

Brand, Chad Owen   *1, 30, 78*

Bruce, F. F.   *16–19, 57, 65, 67*

C

Carey, William   *8, 60*

Creath, S. A.   *15*

D

Dever, Mark   *56–57*

Dockery, David   *9*

E

Edwards, Morgan   *12–13*

Eitel, Keith   *47*

Elliff, Tom   *3*

F

Fesperman, Dan   *17*

Fleming, Rosco Owen   *17*

Fletcher, Jesse   *9, 14*

Floyd, Ronnie   *32*

Furman, Richard   *10–11, 13–14*

G

Gambrell, J. B.   *17–18*

Goheen, Michael   *51–53*

Greear, J. D.   *2*

Grenz, Stanley   *56*

Grissom, Fred   *19*

H

Hall, Gordon   *8*

Hammett, John S.   *44–45, 56*

Hankins, Barry   *1, 22*

Hankins, David   *1, 30, 78*

Hendricks, Shawn   *78*

Hiebert, Paul   *62*

Hunt, Johnny   *32*

J

Johnson, W. B.   *13–14*

Judson, Adoniram   *8*

Judson, Ann   *8*

K

Keathley, Kenneth   *57*

Kittel, Gerhard   *62*

Köstenberger, Andreas J.   *61, 66*

L

Law, Curtis Lee   *21*

Ledbetter, Tammi Reed   *29*

Leonard, Bill   *2*

M

Manly, Basil, Jr.   *56*

Marsden, George   *21*

McBeth, Leon   *3, 7, 9, 10–14, 20, 34–35*

McKnight, Scot   *52*

Mohler, R. Albert   *43–44, 46*

Moon, Charlotte (Lottie)   *36*

Morris, Leon   *70*

Mounce, Robert   *69*

N

Newell, Samuel and Harriett   *8*

Norris, J. Frank   *22*

P-O

O'Brien, Peter T.   *61, 66*

P

Page, Frank   *79*

Pipes, Carol   *40*

Platt, David   *2*

R

Rainer, Thom   *47*

Rice, Luther   *8–10*

Roach, David   *2, 34*

Russell, Allyn   *22*

S

Scarborough, L. R.   *22–23*

Smith, Andrew C.   *20–21*

Stott, John   *42, 58*

Stow, Baron   *11*

T

Toalston, Art   *2*

Torbet, Robert A.   *11*

W-Z

Wayland, Francis   *10–11*

Wills, Greg   *45*

Wooddell, Joseph D.   *44, 46–47*

Wright, Christopher J. H.   *8, 12, 51*

Subject Index

A

Abstract of Principles   56–57
Annie Armstrong Easter Offering   36, 40
Annuity Board   35
Antioch church   66–68
association   10
associationalism   12–13
associational method   11
Augusta, Georgia   1, 3, 35
autonomous   60
autonomy   22, 45, 57, 74, 77, 80

B

Baptist Faith and Message   20, 22–24,
    43–44, 57, 76, 79
Baptist General Convention of Texas   22
Baptist Press   38
Baptist Sunday School Board   35, 39
B&H Publishing Group   39
boll weevil   17
Brotherhood Commission   31

C

Christian Life Commission   31
Congregationalist   8
Conservative Resurgence   30, 42, 79, 81
Convention structure   1, 10–11
Cooperative Baptist Fellowship   30
Cooperative Program   19–20, 25, 71,
    76–77, 83
Council of Seminary Presidents   31, 37
Covenant for a New Century   25, 30, 33, 38

D

disaster relief   29, 36, 82
doctrine of cooperation   20, 23–24
Domestic Mission Board   14

E

Education Commission   31
Efficiency Committee   16
Ethics and Religious Liberty
    Commission   27, 31, 34, 38
Executive Committee   26–27, 31, 33–35,
    38, 76, 79, 81

F

Foreign Mission Board   14–15, 31
fundamentalism   21–22, 76
Fundamentalists   21–23

G

Gateway Seminary   37
General Baptists   12
God's mission   49–52, 60, 70–71, 74, 83
Great Commission   3, 31, 36, 84
Great Commission Resurgence   25, 30–31
Great Commission Task Force   29, 31–32,
    34
GuideStone Financial Resources   35, 38

H

Historical Commission   31
Home Mission Board   15–16, 31

91

I

inerrancy   *44–45*

International Mission Board   *2–3, 27, 31, 33–35, 79, 82*

J

Jerusalem Church   *66–68*

L

Landmark Baptists   *56*

LifeWay Christian Resources   *35, 39*

LifeWay Research   *39, 78, 80*

local church   *25–26, 45, 56–57, 59–60, 62–63, 74, 77, 79–80, 83*

Lottie Moon Christmas Offering   *36, 39*

M

messengers   *28*

Midwestern Baptist Theological Seminary   *37*

mission of the church   *3, 55, 63, 70*

Mission Dignity   *39*

mission of God   *3, 40, 80*

modernist/fundamentalist controversy   *20*

N

New Hampshire Confession   *20, 23*

New Orleans Baptist Theological Seminary   *37*

North American Mission Board   *27, 29, 31, 33–34, 79*

O

1% Challenge   *81*

one sacred effort   *53, 55*

P

Philadelphia Association   *12*

Philadelphia Confession   *12*

Program and Structure Committee   *30*

Protestant liberalism   *21*

R

Radio and Television Commission   *31*

Red Cross   *30*

regenerate church membership   *45*

Ridgecrest Conference Center   *39*

S

Sandy Creek Association   *12–14*

Seminary Extension   *37*

Send Cities   *36*

Send Network   *36*

Send Relief   *36*

Seventy-Five Million Campaign   *17–20, 22, 75*

slavery   *7, 9, 75*

Social Gospel   *21*

Social Service Commission   *38*

Societies   *10*

society method   *16*

society structure   *10, 75*

Southeastern Baptist Theological Seminary   *37*

Southern Baptist Historical Library and Archives   *37*

Southern Baptist Theological Seminary   *14, 37, 56*

Southwestern Baptist Theological Seminary   *22, 37*

Sunday School Board   *14*

T

Triennial Convention   *7–13, 75*

U

universal church   *56, 60*

V

Victory Week   *18–19*

W

Woman's Missionary Union   *36, 39*

Scripture Index

Genesis
1:31   *50, 76*
2   *50*
2:17   *50*
3:15   *50, 52*
12   *51*
12:2   *55*
12:3   *51*

Deuteronomy
18:15   *51*

2 Samuel
7   *51*

Isaiah
48:20   *63*
49:6   *63*
53   *51*

Matthew
1:1   *52*
16:18   *56*
28   *61–62*
28:18–20   *60*
28:19   *62*

Mark
16:15–18   *60*

Luke
24   *61*

24:44–49   *60*
24:46–47   *61*
24:47   *62*
24:48   *61*

John
1:29   *52*
20:21   *60*

Acts
1   *61*
1:8   *53, 60–62, 66*
10   *65*
11   *65*
11:18   *65*
11:19–21   *66*
11:23   *66*
11:24   *66*
11:25–26   *66*
11:27   *67*
13   *68*
13:1–3   *68*
13:5, 13   *68*
16   *69*
19:29   *71*
20:4   *71*
27:2   *71*

Romans
5   *50*
5:12   *50*
5:17   *50*

5:18   50–51
5:19   50–51
12   57
15:24   69
15:30–32   70
16:5   56

1 Corinthians
1:2   56
12   57–59
12:4–6   59
12:12–13   59
12:14–25   59

Galatians
1:2   56
2   67
2:1   67
2:2   67
2:6–10   67
3:7   56
6   57

Ephesians
1:5   49
1:9   49
1:10   49, 53
2   57
4   57–59
4:3–5   58
4:11–13   59
5   57

5:23   56

Philippians
1:5   69
2:25   70
4:15–20   69
4:18   70

Colossians
1   57
1:7   71
1:18   56
2:14–15   52
4:10   71
4:12   71

1 Thessalonians
2:7–9   69

2 Thessalonians
3:1–2   70

Philemon
1:23   71
1:24   71

1 Peter
2   57

Revelation
19–20   57